Other Books by Anne LaBastille

WOODSWOMAN

BEYOND BLACK BEAR LAKE
(sequel to WOODSWOMAN)

WOMEN and WILDERNESS

MAMA POC

THE WILDERNESS WORLD of ANNE LaBASTILLE

JAGUAR TOTEM

WOODSWOMAN III

Woodswoman III

Book Three of the Woodswoman's Adventures

Anne LaBastille

WEST OF THE WIND PUBLICATIONS, INC.
Westport, N.Y., U.S.A.

COVER PHOTO: *Anne, Chekika and Xandor snowshoe to cabin over Black Bear Lake.*

Copyright ©1997 by Anne LaBastille. *All Rights Reserved.*

Printed in the United States of America
by Queen City Printers Inc., Burlington, VT.

The names of certain persons in this book have been changed to protect their privacy.
Photos by Author, unless indicated.

Book design and production: Nadine McLaughlin, Jay, N.Y. 12941
The text of this book is composed in Korinna.
This book printed on Plainfield Plus recycled paper.
Cover design by Anne LaBastille.

LIMITED ADIRONDACK EDITION

Permissions given:
"Opening Camp"–adapted from *Adirondack Life*
"Tomboy"–adapted from *Jo's Girls; A Collection of Writings about Tomboys*, Beacon Press, N.Y.
"The Lake That Loved Loons"–adapted from *Bird Watcher's Digest*.

Library of Congress Catalog Card Number: 97-060130
LaBastille, Anne
Woodswoman III, 1st ed.

ISBN 0-9632846-1-4

No part of this publication may be reproduced or transmitted in any form or by any means, electronic, or mechanical, including photocopy, recording, or any information storage and retrieval system now known or to be invented, without permission in writing from the publisher, except by a reviewer who wishes to quote brief passages in connection with a review written for inclusion in a magazine, newspaper, or broadcast.

West of the Wind Publications, Inc., Westport, N.Y., 12993, U.S.A.

8 9 10

To Dr. Dan W. Odell

Professor Emeritus of English

–my literary guru–

Acknowledgements

Every book in its beginning is dependent on a good typist, a good copy editor, and a good printer. How fortunate I was in having all three. My heartfelt thanks go to Mrs. Pat Reinhart and Ms. Lee Kassin for their dedicated typing. Next I owe my appreciation to Ms. Cynthia Ann Berger for her meticulous copy editing. Lastly, it is my pleasure to acknowledge Ms. Sally Matthews of George Little Press for her steady support and helpful data on the printing of this book.

My dogs, Condor, Chekika, and Xandor, and I especially wish to praise our veterinarian, Dr. Diane Dodd, who has seen us through good health and sad times. Also to Dr. Sue Russell, DVM and wildlife rehabilitator, for her special care of Napoleon. My gratitude to three friends: Dean Spaulding for ornithological information; Richard Beamish for environmental know-how; and Douglas Ward, Esq., for legal advice.

Mr. Richard Sypek and Mr. Phil Arsenault, Senior Investigators with the Bureau of Criminal Investigation of the N.Y. State Police, deserve deep appreciation for their expert handling of the arson case on my property. Then to the great optometrist who keeps me writing well with updated reading glasses, my sincere thanks to Dr. Terry Walton.

Last, but not least, I acknowledge Ms. Mary Jane Scott, my high-school chum and a writer, who generously critiqued my book. And, Mrs. Nadine McLaughlin, who did such a swift and superior job on layout and design of *Woodswoman III*.

Contents

	From Author to Reader	11
1	Opening Camp	17
2	Porcupine Predicament	21
3	Cabin Complexities	32
4	An Ol' Book Peddler	41
5	Condor	55
6	The Lake That Loves Loons	71
7	Twister	80
8	Guiding	96
9	Kestrel Crest Farm	115
10	The Farm and the Cabin	126
11	Napoleon's Gift	138
12	A Mouse in my Truck	150
13	Puppy Xandor	161
14	Mr. Xandor	173
15	An Extraordinary Summer	186
16	Albert	205
17	Like a Kestrel	217
18	Anatomy of an Eco-Catastrophe–I	225
19	Anatomy of an Eco-Catastrophe–II	235
20	Closing Camp	245
	Epilogue	253

From Author to Reader

It's always hard for an author to guess what readers may know about her after reading her books. Those of you who have read *Woodswoman* and its sequel, *Beyond Black Bear Lake*, certainly have some notion of my life in a log cabin at the edge of Adirondack wilderness between 1965 and 1986. And you also understand my profession and how constantly I strive to know nature and to teach the public respect for wildlife and wildlands. *Woodswoman III* continues this story during my third decade, 1987 to 1997. That's right. I've lived in the same cabin for thirty years!

Yet for the benefit of new readers, perhaps I should say something about how I got to the Adirondacks and why I wrote the third book in this trilogy.

My lifelong rebellion against conventional life styles and prejudice toward women probably started the day my mother pronounced, "You can't go hiking in the woods!"

I was ten years old and I was stunned.

She went on to say, her large frame pulsing with well-intentioned Teutonic authority, "You can't go camping either!"

Meanwhile my head was thrumming with outdoor visions from the books I'd been reading under the bed covers, each night, page by flashlit page. Books like *Boy with a Pack* by Stephen Meader, *The Yearling* by Marjorie Kinnan Rawlings, and *Wolf* by Albert Payson

Terhune, the great writer of dog stories.

"Why not?" I wailed.

"Girls don't do that!" was her emphatic reply.

Even then her reasoning seemed wrong to me. Call it my French genes; the French love of "Equality, Liberty, and Fraternity"; or the genes inherited from my French ancestors who stormed the Bastille. I was old enough to sense I had to defy this unjust dictate.

So I turned into a fierce little tomboy outdoors, roaming vacant lots, golf courses, and pond shores in suburban New Jersey. I climbed trees, scaled fences, caught polliwogs, and played baseball with neighborhood boys. My parents gave me a big chow, and I named him "Wolf." He went everywhere with me. How delighted we were with each other. Puppy love, cars, and cosmetics were not the center of my world. Nature and animals gave me much more pleasure.

College brought all kinds of liberation. I leaped at fascinating courses in the natural sciences at Cornell University's Department of Natural Resources. Some classes even required hiking, camping, and running a chain saw. I joined a rifle and pistol club, learned to scuba dive, took judo, and began to drive. I lapped up everything.

During a part-time job at a National Audubon Society office, I met Dr. Roger Tory Peterson, the distinguished ornithologist. He kindly autographed my copy of his *A Field Guide to the Birds,* and advised me to continue studying natural history and conservation. He made a tremendous impression. I was able to tell him so and thank him in person when Dr. Peterson presented his National Nature Educator award to me in 1994.

Since I was continually poor as a college student, I needed to work summers and vacations. That need brought me to the Adirondacks and an outdoor job at a rustic lodge. I worked there three summers, fell in love with my boss, married, and became an innkeeper. The skills and work ethic my husband taught me were invaluable. Though I didn't realize it, they were preparing me for a solo life in a remote log cabin, not a hotel. Despite our divorce, I owe my former husband, Morgan Brown, a debt of eternal gratitude. He paved the way for me to be a woodswoman. I told him so in the summer of 1996.

Two Adirondack guides played a big part in teaching me woods lore and guiding. Rob and, later, Rodney were like my make-believe grandfathers—the ones I never knew. Their caring tutelage helped me become a licensed New York State guide in the 1970s. I've been guiding ever since.

Moving into my little hand-built cabin on 22 acres of old-growth forest in 1965 gave me time to build up a reputation as a reliable free-lance writer and ecological consultant. I finally formalized being a tomboy through my independent life style and challenging career. It made for self-esteem, allowed me to take risks, and be more productive professionally. However, along with my individual freedom came growing responsibilities to the environment and to others.

The environmental movement and the feminist movement began about 1970, making my profession even more legitimate and justifying my long quest for women's equality. They have helped me shape the two main messages of this book.

One is to inspire older women—those of my generation who did not grow up with women's liberation—to act with more independence and self-reliance. Some women are still floundering after divorce, still wondering whether to pursue higher education, and still yearning for a satisfying career. To them I say: Become a fierce eco-feminist and care for Planet Earth.

The second is to show—with local, concrete examples—how the destruction of our environment has speeded up, and how fast we are loosing natural resources, clean air and water, even silence. Wild animals and wild places are disappearing faster and faster as motor power increases, technology explodes, and human population increases exponentially.

Dear readers, you'll find this woodswoman changed. She's not as innocent as when she first took up life in the forest. Perhaps you'll think me more cynical, direct, assertive—even tough at times. I've seen that people and nature can be lovely and loving. They can also be violent and violating. And so you'll read in these chapters which cover the highlights of my past ten years.

Will I write another sequel after my fourth decade at the cabin? Who knows. The vital task before me now is to pick and choose with care those conservation challenges, jobs, friends, and dogs I wish to include in my life. I want the remaining years to be mellow and sweet, like fine wine.

WOODSWOMAN III

Brothers and sisters...
Agree with one another.
Live in peace; and
The God of love and peace
Will be with you.

2 Corinthians 13:11

Log cabin and sun deck on a sunny spring day.

1

Opening Camp

The call comes through late on April 30. "Ice is out," drawls Andy, my laconic best friend in the Adirondacks. "At noon today. Road seems okay." A pause.

"I'll help with repairs and hauling boxes up to your cabin." On that note he hangs up. Andy hates phones.

My heart starts racing like that of a caged bird which suddenly finds its door swung open. One of the worst winters of the century is over, and I'm heading for camp! No telling what havoc the high winds of November, four-foot drifts of January, or Siberian supercold of February have wreaked upon my log cabin.

Next morning I'm up at 5:30, worrying about the "what ifs." A comealong and tow chain for what if I veer off the dirt road and bury my truck in a soft shoulder. A propane torch and pry bar for what if the padlock is frozen or my boat is iced onto shore. An ax for what if ice lingers around my dock and I must chop a channel to land. A life vest for what if I fall into the frigid water.

Finally my two German shepherds and I are in the vehicle. We arrow off the Northway and into the Adirondack Park. Fog as white as polyester fluff drifts above lakes black as onyx. That's hot spring sun heating up ice-cold water. This is the year's third and final death. First comes the death of summer's greenery; second, of fall's vibrant colors; and last, of winter's rock-hard ice and packed snow.

    We reach Black Bear Lake, jump out and skip to shore. Tears and euphoria engulf me. A pair of loons floats 200 yards away as if they'd been anchored there since September. It's Nina and Verplanck, our lake's resident couple. I yodel. They answer—my first welcome home.

    How lucky I am to feel this way about homecoming in a world where millions return to elevators and nondescript apartments that offer no sense of belonging. Where no loons greet and confirm one's harmony with nature.

    Eager to be on the water, I easily unlock my boat, flip it over and slide it into the lake. Wrassling the motor onto the transom, I give three cranks. *Eco!* Chekika and Condor leap in and point like bowsprits as we take off. It seems I'm the first one on the lake this spring—a point of enormous pride. Only one good neighbor is back, deeply tanned from a Florida winter. He lives on the dirt road, so he really doesn't count, does he?

    Halfway up the lake I notice many broken treetops along the shore. The woods streaking by are winter worn, beaten, bleak. Not a trace of green shows at this elevation. A canoe has been smashed. A dock tilted. A neighbor's camp has actually exploded outward from the snow load. I dock the boat and walk apprehensively up my trail. The cabin stands intact!

    My min-max thermometer registers $-38°$ and $93°F$, with present air temperature at 62. Gingerly I unlock the door. The aroma of wool Navajo rugs, balsam pillows, and cold ashes in the wood stove wafts out. I draw in the smells hungrily. At once I light the fire that's been waiting to glow since last fall. After opening windows to help warm the icebox interior, I fly back outdoors to look for damages. The dogs race ahead of me, going from outbuilding to outbuilding, sniffing wildly.

Opening Camp

The north wind has ripped off the plastic that swathed my lean-to. Its floor is still wet from melted snow. Squirrels have gnawed a new hole in the mattress. No big deal. At the outhouse, a huge pine limb lies alongside, having gouged a nick in the roof. Inside the hole is filled with ice. Under the cabin roof lies a three-foot snow pile. No need to light the gas refrigerator—I'll keep groceries in a snow hollow.

I check my long-departed Pitzi's grave. Still shrouded in snow. Come Memorial Day I'll carpet my beloved dog with wildflowers. The woodshed top is atangle with branches. Easy to sweep clean. I carry yellow birch logs indoors, then stoke the fire. The cabin is mellowing. Those cheery flames remind me to fetch water.

On the dock I stand still and soak in the silence. I fill two pails and kneel for my first drink of wild water in six months. It's probably the cleanest water this side of Montana. I scoop up several swallows. The pH be damned. *Giardia* be damned. In over two decades here I've never gotten sick. That ritual over, I lug the pails up to the cabin. Beside the trail, in the same thicket where I saw him last spring, a winter wren is belting out his melody—my second welcome home.

Time to think of tranquil time as sunset nears. And dinner. I slide a precooked casserole into my small gas oven and step outside to turn on the propane tanks. Praying that no lines have cracked in the severe cold, I sniff along the system until sure all's safe. While supper is warming Chekika and Condor eye me expectantly. I feed them extra, knowing how hungry the mountain air and exercise has made them. Then I plug in my phone, hoping it works, and call Andy. He promises to come in the morning to help unload my truck and ferry the gear to camp.

Late light dancing off the lake turns my log room golden. I sweep up some mouse droppings and pick up two books toppled by a trespassing squirrel. In the sleeping loft, I discover old birdseed hidden in my wool blankets. Such is the extent of interior damages. No real repairs are needed.

I head down to the dock carrying an Adirondack chair and snuggle into it. A winter down jacket and the steaming dinner on my lap warm me inside and out. The sun sets behind bare trees. Two white gulls wheel overhead. Not a sound. I contemplate my good fortune after this horrific winter. Seems to me that Nature tempered her fury predictably with protective snows, strong trees, thick ice. She's brought the earth full circle to feel the caress of a warm sun again. All the forest refuse and litter will slowly turn into rich duff. Green plants and bright birds shall soon return.

Yet it also seems to me that Nature deals out as much chaos as predictability. Why was my neighbor's camp flattened—but not mine? Why was another neighbor's woodshed canted cockeyed? Why was someone else's canoe smashed—but not my three? This wild winter treated my property and cabin kindly. The next may not...

A barred owl hoots across the lake so chill—my third welcome home.

2

Porcupine Predicament

A dusting of snow fell overnight and I awoke to an overcast, chilly day. It looked and felt like November. No matter. It was May first and it was spring. I was back home. Soon all my belongings would be under one roof. Quickly I donned the same clothes and worn sneakers from the day before. I called Andy and found him ready to leave. We are both such early risers. I threw on my down jacket and headed to the public dock to meet my friend.

We emptied the truck, loaded the boat, and brought everything up to the cabin. By noon boxes of

Anne and dogs head home loaded with boxes of books, suitcase, dog food, and a huge fern. *Photo by Jennie Bruyn*

books, tools, groceries, dog food bags, files, and clothing had been put away. We ate our sandwiches companionably by the crackling wood stove, chatting casually and catching up on news. Andy's clean-shaven face glowed with ruddy health. His hands and boots looked as comfortably work-worn as ever. And his warm brown eyes held a contentment few men show. He loved the Adirondacks, his woodsy life, his three grown daughters, and his circle of devoted friends. Like me, Andy had been a great fan of Rodney, my beloved forest mentor, and the last of the great old guides, who died in 1989. Andy had often worked with him.

After lunch I suggested we carry the rest of my Adirondack chairs, spool tables, and mailbox from where they were stored onto my sundeck and dock. "They'll make the place look more inviting while waiting for summer," I explained.

"Sure thing," he said.

Happily walking along the trail ahead of Andy, with a chair upside down on my head, I crossed a thin patch of snow. Abruptly my right sneaker slid down a small incline. Snap! I fell backwards on my behind, throwing the chair to one side, and felt a searing pain shoot up my leg. One look and I knew my ankle was badly sprained.

Andy turned pale. He put down his chair and rushed to my side. "Ankle?" he asked. "God, I heard it."

I nodded, rocking back and forth as shock started.

"Those sneakers!" he exclaimed. "No good on snow."

"I know, I know," I groaned, "but it was 62 degrees yesterday so I wore them. They're my favorites. I never dreamed it would snow last night and then not melt right away."

"What shall I do?" Andy asked anxiously.

I thought hard for a moment. Did I really want to beg him for help? To go to his home and be taken care of for several days? I knew from past sprains that I'd be unable to walk for perhaps a week, even with a bandage. How would I manage at the cabin? I couldn't carry pails of water, tote armloads of firewood, climb into my sleeping loft, or. . .or. . .even go to the outhouse. This rustic home of mine was really designed for the hale and hardy.

On the other hand, I had bags of tasty groceries, plenty of dog food, desk work to do, and books to read. My wood stove was new and toasty; my sleeping bag was warm. Most of all I was home where I'd yearned to be for six long months—where my heart belonged. Being unable to walk didn't seem that critical by comparison.

"Andy," I said swiftly, "I have a window of half an hour, maybe 45 minutes, to get settled and secured here. Will you scurry around as fast as you can? Let me give the orders? Then you take the boat down and go on home."

His face creased with concern. "You *sure?*"

"I'll be okay. It's just going to be slow going. If I need you, I'll call. You can be here in no time."

I was drawing on the experience of other accidents. The broken pelvis I'd sustained back in the woods in 1974. That one turned out to be a godsend. Those four months of not being able to walk had allowed me to write *Woodswoman*. Years later I'd ripped the quadriceps muscle on my left leg. But I had to care for my crippled dog, Condor. That accident had an unhappy ending. Both times I'd been alone. Both times had been rough. But I knew I could do it again.

"Help me up, Andy, and let's boogie!"

He supported me into the kitchen, where I swallowed three aspirins. The real pain hadn't begun yet. "First, please bring me a pail of lake water. I'll start soaking the ankle immediately." I sank down in my desk chair and propped my right leg on the desk top.

When he came back with the pail, I stuck my bare foot in and winced. It was cold.

"Better fill all the pails you can find with water," I continued. "One for the dogs on the floor, one for me to drink by the sink. One to cook with and wash dishes on the stove. Then leave two half-full pails by the back door. I can go to the bathroom in them. If waste is diluted with water and a little bleach, it doesn't get offensive for two or three days. I'll cover the pails with newspapers and figure out how to empty them later."

I thought of another task. "After that you better pile as much wood as possible near the wood stove and more right out the back door.

Andy looked at me skeptically. "This won't be clean or comfortable for you," he grumbled. "How're you going to wash?"

I smiled wanly, for the ankle was swelling now. "I'll just have to be a dirty bird for a week. Won't kill me."

He bustled around energetically while I managed to lay a camping mattress, pillows, and sleeping bag on the cabin floor next to the stove.

"Would you feed the dogs before you go?" I begged. "It'll save me some hopping."

"You bet."

When he finished all this, Andy went out to the woodshed and brought back two stout beaver sticks about six feet long. I had been saving them to make hiking poles. "You'll need these," he prophesied. "How's it feel?"

"Numb. I'm going to lie down now and try to get warm. I still feel a little shocky. Could you set my battery radio and phone on the floor, please? What a dear you are."

That window of time was closing fast. He covered me up with two extra wool blankets, stoked up the stove, and looked around the cabin. "You've got all the things you need right at your fingertips, Anne. But call if you want anything at all."

I nodded and blew him a kiss. "Leave the dogs inside." Then I shut my eyes. The back door closed. A couple of minutes later, I heard the outboard motor start and drone down the lake.

Alone. I was finally alone in my cabin four miles from the nearest person by water and road—incapacitated. This was surely turning out to be the most unusual homecoming in all my years. I still felt cold, so I sat up, swivelled around in my bag, and grabbed a log. I could easily open the stove door and feed the fire. The heat gradually calmed my racing pulse and I dozed until dark. The pain woke me. I crawled on hands and knees to the back door, let my dogs out for a minute, peed in a pail, and crawled back to my bag. Those shepherds sensed something was amiss and lay down close by me. It was a rocky night.

Next morning my ankle was almost the size of a grapefruit. It looked frightful, but I resolved not to call my doctor. All he'd do was advise RICE—rest, ice, compression, elevation—as I knew from my first aid and EMT training. I could do these things myself. Besides, now I couldn't even get to the health center. My boat was at the far end of the lake, and I never could have driven or braked my truck with that right foot.

I hopped into the kitchen and propped myself on a stool. Making a hot espresso, I swallowed more aspirins to stop the throbbing. Idly, I stared out the window. Suddenly I saw a huge porcupine waddle past my woodshed, just ten feet away, and into the fir forest behind the camp. He didn't know I was there, and the dogs hadn't been out yet. His quills were folded down close to his body. He peered near-sightedly here and there. Totally unperturbed. Off for a morning's stroll to chew some tree bark and pine needles. Where had he come from?

Imagine! Just imagine, I groaned inwardly, if I'd let Chekika and Condor outdoors three minutes earlier! They would have run right into the "quill pig." There'd have been the devil to pay. Condor was a veteran of three encounters with porcupines and had taken nearly 50 quills. He never would have let this one past him without getting stuck some more. And Chekika, quick and nimble as she was, might easily have gotten a snootfull just to rival her father. It would have been her first experience; however, it would certainly have been her last. She was too smart to repeat such a stunt.

A dog with quills in its face and mouth usually goes berserk: shakes its head, swipes with its paws, rubs against trees or people, snaps its teeth and runs around. It does anything to loosen those little pointed arrows. Being barbed at the tip, however, the quills stay embedded. Snipping off the quill's end does not deflate the quill and barb nor make removal easier. In fact this old-fashioned practice makes it much harder to grasp quills as they work deeper into an animal's flesh. There are only two ways to get them out. One is have a vet anesthetize the animal and withdraw them with surgical tweezers. The other method is to wrap a dog in heavy blankets and hog-tie it with a rope. Then find a friend to sit on the dog, put a stick between its jaws so as not to get bitten by mistake, and start pulling quills out with pliers. Painful for the dog and nerve-racking for the owner. But it works in the wilderness.

In my present condition I could do neither. I'd have to call Andy or the fire department, and deal with two half-crazed dogs until someone arrived. What terrible timing. I would need to be extra careful about letting them out every time. I crawled out the back door with a large aluminum pot and cover, sat on the ramp, and banged the two together, making quite a racket. I waited a few moments to give the slow-moving creature time to climb a tree—if he was in earshot—and then let the dogs outside. In five minutes I blew two blasts on their dog whistle. They came running back with no quills showing.

I crawled on all fours in to my desk and levered myself onto the chair. Condor and Chekika looked at me quizzically. "What a way to start the day, boys," I said. "I'm going to be a dog now and join your world."

It was a demanding world. I'd crawl to the lake twice a day, splash my face, take a drink, and fill two plastic milk jugs with water. While on the dock, I'd soak my purple ankle in that 38-degree lake until all pain left. Then I'd crawl back to the camp with the jugs tied behind me on a rope and deposit them inside. Next I dragged firewood, two logs at a time, behind me in a laundry bag. When a waste pail began to smell, I'd crawl on my knees to the nearest large spruce with holes among the roots and empty it there. Later I could cover the waste with fresh dirt. It was tedious, frustrating labor just to move and to handle my three most essential needs for survival: water, heat, and waste.

Being a dog was also visually *very* boring. Dogs really only see the world from the ground up to three or four feet. They rarely look at the sky, or into trees, or much above their owner's eyes. It's due to the anatomy of their necks and position of their heads. At least that's how my head and neck reacted. Also dogs rely on smell, sounds, and night vision to augment their black-and-white world—but I couldn't. At least I saw in color and that made things more interesting. But with only one leg working instead of four, it was very boring indeed.

Despite these days of crawling chores and the painful injury, I had a marvelous week at my cabin. The early May weather turned warm and clear. Time slowed way down. I would crawl onto my sun deck and sit in the sun for hours, just as Thoreau had done in his doorway. I wrote and read as long as I liked. There were no leaves to block the rays and no black flies. Wave after wave of spring migrants arrived, and the woods rang cheerily with their songs. I could indulge my passion for bird watching to the fullest.

With binocs and bird book on my lap, I'd *shuuuush* and squeak the birds near and identify them. Black-throated blues, yellow-rumped, magnolia, and blackburnian warblers called from still-bare tree tops. An ovenbird emphatically repeated himself over and over: *teacher, teacher, teacher*. He scuttled among last year's dry leaves where fuzzy green fiddle heads were pushing up. A pair of common yellowthroats jumped about in the shoreline thickets, chanting *witchy, witchy, witchy, witch*. A pileated woodpecker pounded a spruce trunk on the hill. The sound echoed like a jackhammer across the lake. Robins, grackles, rose-breasted grosbeaks were all around.

Late in the day, timed perfectly with my afternoon ankle soak, the loon pair sedately swam by in slow motion without a ripple or sound. The water was as black as their heads and necks. Their white marbled backs, wide white "necklaces" and small white throat patches were stunningly reflected.

"Quite a recovery room," I quipped aloud to the dogs.

And I really didn't mind my ankle much after the third day. The swelling went down, and by wrapping a large Ace bandage around it, I could hop here and there with my beaver sticks. Throughout that week Chekika stayed at my side, acting like a "nurse dog." She stayed near the back door, looking at me, while Condor roamed around importantly marking his territory. Then at night she'd lie curled against my tummy. I tickled her lovely champagne-colored ears, stroked her fawn guard hairs, and called her my love.

I phoned Andy every evening and assured him I was managing beautifully. "It's like rediscovering birds, springtime, silence, and life as it used to be back in the sixties."

"Anyone else around?" he asked.

"Not a soul," I replied. "I'm sitting in 'God's pocket.'"

On the fourth night I heard a rummaging noise under the cabin. It came from the space enclosed by latticework where I store cardboard boxes, sand, short

Porcupine Predicament

sections of lumber, plastic pipe and a large, empty garbage pail. Nothing to eat there. I lay awake wondering if it was a bear or coon or even the porcupine. The dogs whined restlessly, but it seemed too risky to go out and investigate.

The fifth night was the same. This time my curiosity won. Suspecting it might be the quill pig from the chewing sounds, I put both dogs on leashes and gave them a stern lecture on the potential dangers. After putting a small flashlight in my pocket, I carefully hopped out the door. Obediently, Condor and Chekika followed. They didn't pull me over or rush under the camp. Very slowly we sneaked up to the narrow opening and I shined the light in. There sat the largest porcupine I'd ever seen on top of my metal garbage pail. He must have weighed 25 to 30 pounds. His tiny shoe-button eyes, set so close together, reflected the light like two pieces of shiny coal. His nostrils twitched delicately as he scented us. He did a little shuffle atop the lid. Nervous. The dogs whined eagerly, but I kept a tight hold of the leashes with one hand while I clasped the side of the cabin with the other.

"BE CAREFUL!" I told them in a no-nonsense voice.

I now had the pleasure of examining a quill pig at close range. He couldn't squeeze out of the space except at the opening where we stood. The dogs couldn't get in, the opening being so small. We eyeballed one another curiously.

The porky's mouth had black lips that looked to me like a petulant child's, pursed up to cry. I glimpsed the bright orange teeth that can gnaw on trees or graze on grass. His head was quite small and narrow compared to his big body. Most of his size, I guessed, was due to the raised quills. A porcupine may sport up to 30,000! This animal was definitely on the defensive, as his spikes were standing straight up. They would be a sure mine field for the dogs. His paws had long, curved nails, superb for climbing trees. They looked like they might make nasty weapons, too. With his black-and-white fur and quills, this porcupine was every bit as handsome as those loons. Yet I felt a frailness and pathetic quality showed in its face. I recalled how slowly porkies move, how poor their vision is said to be. I recalled the dozens and dozens I've seen run over by cars. They are absolutely defenseless on roadways.

I thought back to the professor who taught wilderness packing and outfitting at Colorado State University. He told us that porkies are the one species in the North Woods that lost or starving people can manage to kill and eat. He had killed and cooked a porcupine for our class. To me the meat tasted like balsam needles. Who would want to eat that poor thing, except in extreme desperation?

Meanwhile the porky was moaning in the high, querulous manner of his kind. It made me yearn for a baby porcupine to raise so gently that it would never lift a quill to me. I looked around the space under the cabin to see what had attracted the animal. I'd left six or seven long pressed-cardboard rollers there last fall, the kind that go inside a roll of carpet. Very strong. I thought they might come in handy for moving a heavy object some day. Not anymore. The porcupine had gnawed all the six-foot-long rollers down to two feet. Strewn all over the ground were his dark, oval, pellet-like droppings. So this was his winter delicatessen, and the metal garbage can lid his motel bed.

My dogs were standing very still, registering every move with antenna ears, moist black noses, and night-adjusted eyes. They were being very good. I repeated "BE CAREFUL" and admonished them not to charge. Then I hopped backward to the ramp and pulled Condor and Chekika indoors with me.

Next morning our guest was gone. I called Andy to pick me up by boat so I could see my GP about the ankle. It was healing too slowly, I thought, and I was tired of being a dog. The doctor clucked sympathetically, applied an air cast, and ten minutes later I walked out without a bandage or beaver stick. True, I waddled a bit like a porcupine, but I was mobile again.

Life moved back into the fast lane now that I could drive, run my boat, and use two legs. The next day the first boatload of summer people motored up the lake, the couple dwarfed by their load of belongings. I waved to them from my dock.

"Hope their homecoming won't be as prickly as ours," I muttered to the dogs.

3

Cabin Complexities

Half of the people who send me fan mail and half of the people who speak to me after lectures and book signings express envy at my life. They imagine I do little else except write, read outdoor books, and guide in the woods. They fantasize that I have long blocks of quiet time when I wax poetic or contemplate nature. Life in a log cabin at the edge of wilderness seems the culmination and epitome of a simple, tranquil, and leisurely way of life.

Seldom do I try to convince them otherwise. They wouldn't believe it unless they could be there to see me scurry around. Also, they are right, in part. The early days at my cabin were extremely peaceful and productive. I had all morning to write—and all afternoon to chop wood, paint roofs, shovel snow, repair gear, or go canoeing. Evenings did hold hallowed hours when I read, played with my dogs, sewed balsam pillows, and listened to the radio. Yet I was always driven by poverty to work, work, work; write, write, write. This industriousness changed my life style little by little.

Now—oh, oh, oh—if one of my fans dropped in between 6:00 and 7:00 A.M. and spent the day observing cabin life, she or he might not believe the pace, complexities, and problems. Like many entrepreneurs, I'm driven by the world I created and the demands of making a living.

Wake-up time: Around 6:00 A.M., Puppy Xandor

Cabin Complexities

licks me on the mouth, nose, and eyes, wolf-fashion. He makes sure I stand up so the day can start. I put on his collar. Chekika rubs against my legs affectionately and I slip on her collar, too. I take a few moments to brew a tiny cup of espresso before we hurry to the "office." It's a long ways back in the woods and it takes some time to get there. The coffee is all gone by the time we arrive. This small shed allows me, via a power line, to operate a fax, phone machine, copier, even a battery charger, which all help streamline my business.

Communications time: I send any necessary faxes to Central America (where I still continue research at Lake Atitlán) and Europe (where I occasionally lecture) before 7:00 A.M., when the international tariffs change from the night rate to the high business rate. Often there are delays, jammed documents, mis-dials, and other obstructions across those thousands of miles. I may have to stop at 7:00 A.M. and wait until the next morning. Between 7:00 and 8:00 A.M. I make domestic long distance faxes and calls, taking advantage of United States night rates which run from 11:00 P.M. until 8:00 A.M. Now I'm ready to walk back via the outhouse. I sit there a few minutes, admiring my huge virgin white pine and listening to bird calls. Usually there's a tiny winter wren trilling his rollercoaster song nearby.

Breakfast time: Returning to the cabin, I fix dog chow mixed with meat for Chekika and Xandor. I set another espresso to brew while I lather cream cheese and homemade jam on a slice of dark bread. I've now been up for two hours.

Desk time: Because I'm a morning person, it's imperative that I use my brain power between roughly 8:00 A.M. to 1:00 or 2:00 P.M. After that it fails, like a faucet of water turned down to a trickle. Years ago I could afford to fuss and fiddle with a manuscript for five or six hours. Now, sad to say, 50 percent of that time is taken up with correspondence, bills, and administrative details.

My invisible observer would peer at the piles of papers littering my desk and wonder what kind of details could take so long. Well, certain essentials like New York State quarterly sales taxes on books I've sold. Infernal IRS forms and bookkeeping. Dog licenses, rabies vaccinations, heartworm checks. Vehicle inspection, registrations, insurances, and licensing for a truck, two boats, and one trailer. Appointments for oil change and lube, rotating tires, and maintenance work. Appointments for my maintenance, too, like dentist, endodontist, mammograms, pap smears, eye tests, new glasses, and doctors for the occasional injury. Then the blue maze of Blue Cross. Bills, bills, bills. Chain saw repairs and sharpening. Books to be autographed, wrapped, shipped, and invoiced. Ads to be placed for my guiding service. Manuscripts sent by publishers asking for a favorable book blurb or review. My writing workshops to be booked and prepared for. Conservation organizations pleading for donations. Students or friends begging for letters of recommendation. Extra-nice fan mail. Every single detail carries its own deadline and its own penalty for ignoring that.

One winter, for example, I nicked my shin while shoveling three feet of snow from the roof at Thoreau II. I paid no attention to this minor cut and didn't even cleanse or cover the wound. A week later, I had to stop work and drive 100 miles round trip to an emergency care facility, wait an hour to be examined, purchase antibiotics, and spent $55. I felt horrible.

One spring, I forgot to pay the sales tax on my book sales in time, so I raced 25 miles to the post office, spent six dollars for Priority Certified Mail, was fined a $50 late fee, and felt grouchy as a spring bear.

By now I've been up for four hours and my main goal—to write—has not yet been realized.

Mail time: The mail boat comes by each morning at 10:30 A.M. The importance of this visit cannot be over-

Cabin Complexities

estimated. Having such government service on this isolated backcountry lake is really amazing, although it only functions for ten weeks. Nevertheless, the time, gas, oil, and energy I save by having mail picked up and dropped off is a boon. I rush to finish any important correspondence and shove everything in a large, old, gray canvas bag. I must remember to insert money to pay for these mailings or the post office won't send it on. As soon as the dogs hear the motorboat coming, they race to the dock and bark loudly. At 11:00 A.M. the mail boat returns with a new batch of correspondence which threatens to curtail my writing time even more.

Quickly, I slice open envelopes and deal with any urgent matters. Invariably I need to make a long-distance call, or the phone rings. I feel my temper fraying. Twenty-five years ago I was lucky to receive a dozen letters a week and no calls. Today, it's a dozen letters a day and up to 30 calls a week. Every morning about this time, I think back to how splendid it was when no phone linked me to the outer world. Sure, it was rough sometimes having to travel out by boat, canoe, snowshoe, or snowmobile to get to my truck and then drive miles to the post office or a public phone booth. Yet the feeling of being in control of my day and flowing from task to task was worth it. Now I feel my professional life is out of control. I've learned that published writers are never in control, due to the barrage of communications and tight deadlines from editors.

Writing time: Finally I have two or three hours in which to write. I avoid interruptions by working outdoors on my sun porch, or sitting in a canoe, under a shady tree, or at the bottom of my motorboat. I use only a yellow pad and black pen and a manual typewriter. Oh, Thoreau, how lucky you were, sitting in the doorway of your little cabin all morning, as undisturbed and free as any bird. No wonder *Walden* is such a smashing hit, has endured 150 years, and is published in so many different languages.

Lunch time: My writing spree is ended by pangs of hunger. It's 1:30 P.M. and my brain power has turned off. Dogs and I hurry back to the cabin for a light lunch of cottage cheese and dog biscuits during which I may read personal letters, flip through a catalogue, or pen a postcard. By 2:00 P.M. the dogs and I are like caged tigers. Our limbs long to stretch and our muscles long to flex. Taking as much time as possible, we stay outdoors and enjoy being active.

Free time: We swim, carry wood, burn brush, do repairs, throw balls and sticks, and eventually take another walk back to the "office" to check the machines before 5:00 P.M. I've now been up ten hours.

Desk time: The observer may find me dealing with special problems late in the afternoon. Usually they are caused by others' mistakes. Why is there, I wonder, so much carelessness in the work world of America? Why should the laxness of others end up as *my* cost of doing business?

Take what happened when my self-published book, *The Wilderness World of Anne LaBastille,* came off the press. It looked beautiful—shiny, clean, full-color cover, neatly stacked. That same day I shipped 300 copies to a bookstore waiting for advance sales. I used stout boxes and packing materials. Yet somehow the shipper managed to bang up all those boxes. The rough handling scuffed the covers, bent the edges, and made the 300 copies completely unsalable. This represented, in retail sales, a $1,700 loss. All the books were sent back to me, at my expense, even more battered. Frantic calls to the shipper's office didn't help. The company's insurance only covered $200. So I began a lengthy correspondence with the regional manager and finally with the CEO of the company. Months later, the shipper settled on the wholesale value of the books and sent me a check for roughly $1,000. But it cost me many sales by not having this book in stock. This doesn't include the

Cabin Complexities

phone calls, faxes, letters, and other costs I had to absorb.

All this "busy work" takes quite an emotional toll. I never, ever, realized my life would evolve into this. I chose an isolated cabin to be calm and creative, watch wildlife, soak in Nature. Today it feels as if the world has me by the throat and is dragging me back and forth, gasping, through the woods. By now, the make-believe observer is probably running down a trail or paddling furiously down the lake as fast as she or he can go, muttering, "Let me out of here!" Yet if that person hung on just one or two hours more, she or he might witness a mellower mood with the setting sun.

At 7:00 P.M. I shut the phone off. The dogs and I make one last trip to check for faxes and messages. As we stroll back through the woods, shadows are lengthening. A hush fills the forest. A solitary hermit thrush pipes pure harmonics behind the office. This sound is so pure, so eloquent, so like crystal that I stop, sit down on a log, and tremble at his song. The canopy above is golden green against a cobalt sky, shimmering with shafts of horizontal sun. A few leaves tremble—or are they also reacting to that spot-breasted, dove-grey ventriloquist's music?

As the sun edges behind the hills, I sink into an Adirondack chair on my dock in a ritual I've obeyed since building the cabin. This is when I shift gears. When I give thanks for another productive and beautiful Adirondack day. Wavelets turn turquoise and saffron. A beaver slaps its tail. The first bat zings down to the water. Mergansers float by. The loons call softly.

Maybe I'll write a beloved friend while sitting on my dock, or do a bit of reading. More likely, I'll burrow into my sleeping bag with a thriller right after supper and read by candlelight. The dogs will curl beside me. A stray thought drifts through my mind. Could it be, I ponder, that someday I'll be replaced or phased out by modems, computer manuscripts, laser print-outs, or more complicated machinery? So be it. Maybe then I'll once again feel like a complete woodswoman.

Thanks heavens I don't own a computer, or I'd be chained to an electric outlet, dodging E-mail, watching the World Wide Web, and maybe trying to write something in my "spare time." I find a phone, phone machine, fax, and copier are devilish enough. So I'm just going to keep on writing with my brain, hand, pen, yellow pad, and manual typewriter.

Looking back, it seems strange how machinery sneaked into my life. After my first book, *Woodswoman*, was published in 1976 and gained popularity, I quickly wrote two more—*Assignment: Wildlife* and *Women and Wilderness*—all produced with my archaic methods. Also, I began supplying some small local shops with my books since it was easier for me than for the shopowners to order them direct. Before long, the little desk I wrote at (a sheet of plywood over two filing cabinets) was far too cluttered to be efficient. Also, I was piling up boxes of books in my cabin for subsequent distribution, until barely enough room remained for me and two dogs.

To add more space I put insulation around the front porch and doubled up on the plexiglass in the picture window. I set up another plywood desk out there—strictly for book writing. The view was toward my huge companion spruce. The desk inside my studio was strictly for correspondence. Then I closed in the space under my cabin where porcupines once snoozed and created a five-foot-high basement with rough shelves where files and books could be stored.

Shortly after these changes, I brought in a phone line via underwater cable. I set an old red rotary phone on the desk. Now I needed space for phone books and note paper. The phone was useful, all right, but it drove me nuts! Eventually I learned to put limits on its hours, got an unlisted number, and did not let it gain the upper hand. I answer from 7:00 A.M. to 7:00 P.M, but never at

Cabin Complexities

night. How I delight in turning off that phone ringer!

The thought of a phone machine to shield me and to screen calls stayed in the back of my mind. Without electricity, however, there seemed no way to run one. And I never want my cabin electrified. So years passed, and my tolerance level to interruptions lessened and lessened.

Then when fax machines came out, they immediately captured my imagination. They would save a lot of money and cut down the time it took to receive a document from *days* for mail delivery to mere *minutes* by fax. I resolved to get one. The problem was still electricity. No way I could run a machine like this on solar or 12-volt batteries.

One day I was in a hardware store and saw a small prefab storage shed on display. Suddenly, the idea of erecting one and using it just for useful office machinery dawned on me. All these years I had had to drive 25 or 50 miles round trip and pay 25 cents a copy just to duplicate a piece of paper or mail a package. I craved the advantages of a personal copier. I deserved it!

The stumbling block was that the power line lay a long way from the lake. I found a piece of flat land where it seemed a small shed could fit. I set up an appointment with the power company to inspect the site. It was quickly approved and the line buried. I bought a prefab shed and had it delivered to the lake. Transporting and erecting this tiny building is a later saga.

At times I crave solitude, or wish to write undisturbed, or just want to jump off life's merry-go-round. So I walk back to my office, shut off everything, and pull the main switch. Then I spend a couple of days at my cabin like it *used* to be.

Recently a dear friend complained bitterly that she had tried to reach me all weekend without the slightest success (no cheery machine message, no friendly fax bird chirp).

"That's right," I said.

"But what if someone really needed to get in touch?" she countered, "or you missed a book sale?"

Using the strongest language I could muster to show my dislike of phones, I said, "*!X¢*#!&+!!!."

I've been driven to it. I'm not escaping responsibility or society. I'm looking out for Number One and for the precious sensibilities which allow me to write. I'm controlling the mechanical invasions of this modern world in order to maintain a small peaceful environment in which to create or contemplate. This is my response to the escalating demands of technology and the threats they impose to my talent.

Ironically, technology has shown me the answer to Thoreau's central question: "How shall we live?"

We must try to keep the realities of owning property and earning money in balance with our Thoreauvian ideals. Be firm, tough, and direct: unplug, switch off, disconnect.

4

An Ol' Book Peddler

A spin-off to my writing-in-the-woods career has been becoming an ol' book peddler. Peddling is very much in the Adirondack tradition. Some of the oldest and best businesses in the mountains began when guides, lumberjacks, and peddlers came here by train or on foot (no roads then). They noticed many amenities were lacking—small hotels, rooming houses, bars, food markets, and hardware stores. Using great ingenuity, they managed to bring the materials needed into the North Woods and open up shop.

One of the prime examples was Moses Cohen, an itinerant Lithuanian Jew, who arrived by ship in New York City as a young man in the late 1800s. His brother owned a hardware store at Bloomingdale in the Adirondack Mountains. Almost penniless, Moses travelled from the metropolis, with a packbasket of belongings on his back, a trip of more than 300 miles to the tiny town. After reuniting with his brother, he decided to walk and hitch buggy rides another 200 miles down to Utica. He got as far as Old Forge and stayed. There he began carrying crucial household and hardware items in his packbasket to the isolated hamlet dwellers. Over the years, he went from an almost penniless peddler to builder and owner of the Old Forge Hardware and the Forge House Inn. The hardware store expanded until today it covers thousands of square feet and offers two million items. Moses' son in turn took over and became a well-to-do entrepreneur and realtor. Now his daughter runs her own store, Wildwood, as well as maintaining a lively interest in the Hardware. Both places offer some of the best collections of Adirondack book titles anywhere in the Park or in the northeast.

These book sections caught my attention in spring 1976. I had seldom gone in any book store, being of the firm opinion that if one wants to write, one writes. Book reading comes second. Now I entered the Hardware to see if *Woodswoman,* published just weeks before, was on the shelves. What a thrill it would be to see my very first book in print. But something was missing. Timidly, I asked the store manager why *Woodswoman* wasn't there.
"What book? What book?" he asked, surprised. "I didn't know you wrote a book, Anne. That's great."
This simple statement changed the course of my life and my attitude as a professional writer. If this friendly local store operator didn't know about *Woodswoman,* who else didn't know? Over the summer, I slowly and tentatively inquired at other shops that sold books. Most combine gifts, curios, maple syrup, antiques, carvings, and cards with their stock. None of them carried *Woodswoman.*
Feeling sheepish, I wrote to my editor to ask what had happened. I had to remind myself that I'd never taken a writing course in college, nor a writing workshop. The extent of my understanding of my book contract was that the publisher sent the writer six complimentary copies of her book after publication. The whole process of book distribution, wholesaling, and promotion was a mystery to me.
The editor replied, "We don't think it would be profitable to send a book rep up there since none of the Adirondack stores are very large. But I can prepare some book flyers for you—a single page with an order blank at the bottom. You can mail these out to

An Ol' Book Peddler

attract customers."

Several days later, a stack of sickly yellow, xeroxed flyers arrived. I mailed these out to every store on my list. Later the kindly hardware manager told me, "Stores can't buy books with *this* form. These are for *individual* sales, for people who want a single copy and make a retail purchase from the publisher."

I looked and felt confused. Had my editor misunderstood me? How did one get books into stores?

"Don't you realize?" the manager said patiently. "Each store has to apply for application forms, then establish credit with the publisher by providing detailed financial data and references. If credit is approved, then, and only then, can a store get a wholesale account and buy books usually at a 40 percent discount. Sales reps only stop in at large stores, which may buy dozens or hundreds of copies at a time. We're way too small for that. Anyway, it's a pain, and most owners up here won't bother establishing credit. Also, I never heard of an author distributing her own book."

"Forty percent?" I exclaimed in astonishment. "You mean you earn 40 percent on the price of each book?"

He nodded affirmatively.

"That's much more than I earn in royalties," I said. "I only get 10 percent on hard cover copies, and 7 percent on soft cover...assuming a book even gets into soft cover. And I'm the one who *wrote* the book. Without me, you wouldn't have anything to sell!"

"Doesn't seem fair, does it?" he murmured sympathetically.

"So how am I going to get *Woodswoman* into Adirondack stores?" I asked. "Sounds like the publishers think there's a black hole up here, or it's the Siberia of America. Or maybe they think no one can read in the woods."

"Guess you'll have to drum up your own business," he said cryptically, and hurried off to help a customer.

I was despondent. That conversation indicated my

wonderful new book would seldom, if ever, be offered in the place where it was most likely to sell. And what about the rest of the country? In a few moments I'd gone from dreaming of a best seller to picturing a remaindered reject.

The peddling idea grew gradually. I began to realize that to give my book a life and earn any money from it at all, I would have to be my book's representative, promoter, and distributor all wrapped into one. But first, I'd have to establish credit with my own publisher, in order to buy wholesale. Twenty years ago authors were discouraged or even prevented from buying their own books at discount. Aside from the six complimentary copies, authors had to buy their own books at retail just like any other customer. The only exception seemed to be for lecture appearances, and then the publisher might try to provide copies direct to a local bookstore. Thus, I seemed to get nowhere with my initial request to market *Woodswoman* in the Adirondacks.

Luckily, I had recently established a for-profit, single-owner, sub-chapter S corporation called West of the Wind Publications, Inc. Because it was a legitimate business and I was president (and every other title of officer), my publisher could not refuse to sell to it. So that's how I obtained my first box of *Woodswoman* wholesale. (Nowadays the profit motive is so strong that it's easy to obtain books; and the more you buy, the bigger the discount.)

Of course I took the first copies to my friend at Old Forge Hardware. I wrapped them carefully and carried them in an old Adirondack packbasket. This seemed fitting for an ol' book peddler. Proudly I laid them out on a large table.

"Please sign them, Anne," said the manager. "Your books might sell a little better if they were autographed."

And they did. A mild curiosity grew about *Woodswoman*. Before long I was getting repeat orders.

An Ol' Book Peddler

I contacted a few other stores and sold them autographed copies, too. The next summer I was asked to do a book signing—my first. Pitzi (my German shepherd brought from Guatemala) stood by the table as I autographed. Half the people wanted his inky paw print next to my scrawl.

From that humble beginning, I went on to garner shelf space in almost 40 shops throughout and surrounding the Adirondack Park. *Woodswoman* is still being sold nationally through the publisher's efforts; however, I believe my early Adirondack initiative is what made the difference in its track record. My first book has sold close to 150,000 copies over 20 years and appeared in three foreign editions. It has hardly made me rich, though, despite the public's fantasy that all writers are millionaires. Actually, only 5 percent of all writers ever make it big time. My royalties, having started at only 37 cents per book, are still less than a dollar a copy. Yet sales are steady and there have been at least 15 printings.

My other six books have not done as well, yet all are in print except for *Assignment: Wildlife*. That one really bombed out. Less than two years after its publication, it was remaindered and disappeared (marked down from $10.95 per hard cover copy to $1.25)! No advertising was ever given the book (same as with *Woodswoman*). No editor advised me of the remaindering decision. No one suggested I buy books up for future lectures and book appearances. I only learned of its disposition by mere luck and managed to purchase the remaining copies at great financial hardship. Once, later on, I came upon a copy in a store's bin of rejects. It lay tattered, worn, faded—victim of a publisher's neglect. I felt a few stray tears fall on that volume before I snatched it up like a lost child and took it home to a more dignified and loving setting on my cabin shelves.

Peddling my books today is hard work, quixotic,

and fun. Every May I visit most of 40 shops in and around the Park. The few that are the farthest away I may contact by phone and mail. I never know what to expect in sales, so I stock up with hundreds of all my titles in late March. It's a hefty expenditure—all based on the hope of good summer weather and lots of tourists. Some orders take four days to arrive; others, a month. No way to plan. Sometimes one title is out of print, and I have to wait until the season is almost over for copies. No editor has ever forewarned me of this or carefully scheduled a new edition in time for the peak of tourist season in the Adirondacks.

Shopkeepers and book buyers also can be capricious. The summer of the Adirondack Park Centennial, 1992, everyone wanted dozens of my books. "Fill me up now for Memorial Day weekend, and repeat the order just before July 4th, okay?" shopkeepers said. (It was a good year.)

The next spring, I heard, "Oh, just leave two of each, Anne. I had to replace my roof this winter and don't have much money for stock." Or, "The recession has finally hit here. Think I'll wait till the end of June to order, but thanks for stopping in."

Then an occasional ungracious buyer might mutter, "Hey, that new book of yours about that crazy bird in Central America doesn't move at all. People only want to read about the Adirondacks. Don't leave any more of those." (It doesn't matter that *Mama Poc* was chosen one of the 14 best environmental books in the 1990s by the Sustainable Futures Society. And that it had smashing reviews in *Smithsonian* magazine and *Wild Earth* journal. Or that it represents 25 years of my life trying to save an endangered species from extinction.)

So it goes, day after day, along my route. A few marvelous markets do exist, such as the Adirondack Museum at Blue Mountain Lake and the Old Forge Hardware. How I love to hear, "I'll take a case of *Woodswoman,* half a case each of *Beyond Black Bear*

An Ol' Book Peddler

Lake and *Women and Wilderness*, and a dozen *The Wilderness World of Anne LaBastille*. Be sure to autograph them, please, Anne." In half an hour I've sold 70 to 75 copies!

I enjoy making book peddling trips and consider many of these shopkeepers my friends. Sometimes we drink coffee and gossip. Before Memorial Day the tempo is slow and there's time to socialize. I crisscross the 100- by 125-mile Park for about ten days. Often I reminisce about how my borders have expanded. When I first came to work in the Adirondacks as a college student, and while I was married, my entire world

Anne and Chekika stayed up all night, watching pages of her new, self-published book, *The Wilderness World of Anne LaBastille,* roll off the press.

Being a book peddler is fun. Anne crisscrosses the Adirondack Park in her truck, distributing books by day and camping out by night.

revolved around our rustic inn and lake. All my social ties lay within a 25-mile radius. Shopping and medical help were found exclusively in Utica. Tupper Lake, Lake Placid, Elizabethtown were dimly recognized names that I'd never been to and doubted I'd ever visit. Little if any homogeneity existed among the 105 hamlets and villages of the Adirondacks. The Park's "Blue Line" was only a mark on the map rather than the friendly frontier to an incredibly beautiful, diverse, and wild region where like-minded independent folk lived.

Twenty years later I know practically every tiny town and hundreds of people along the winding, forested roadways within the six-million-acre Park. The whole place really is "my big backyard."

On warm sunny evenings after dropping off books, I often stop near a wild lake rather than go home to the cabin. Grabbing my tent, sleeping bag, and food, the dogs and I hike to a secluded shoreline. I'll never forget the sandy beach I once found on an uninhabited pond. It faced east and had a fire ring in place, two loons cruising offshore, magnificent pines on an island, and a full moon about to rise. After supper, I pulled my canoe off the truck top and carried it back to the beach.

An Ol' Book Peddler

Chekika, Condor and I paddled serenely around the entire shoreline, gliding past glimpses of a silvery spring moon behind jutting pine limbs and newly leafed birches. Then we slid through black shadows cast by a giant erratic on shore or a low hill. Spring peepers filled the warm air with their warbling love songs. Barred owls hooted companionably from a swamp.

Back on the beach beside my campfire, I thought sadly of other salespeople lying in strange and lonely motels, watching TV, sipping scotch, exhausted from ten hours on the road.

Next morning the rising spring sun warmed my beach enough to swim—first time since October. I ate, fed the dogs, reloaded the canoe, and set off peddling with a light heart. Sue Hubbell, author of *A Country Year* and peddler of honey from her Ozark cabin, has nothing on me, I thought. She had to sleep in her pick-up at the edges of Manhattan with cartons of precious honey piled in back. I leave my boxes of books in the truck and take my pick of almost 3,000 lakes and ponds and huge tracts of wild forests for my bedding-down spot.

One day I was driving along a remote stretch of road in the eastern Adirondacks. The forest was spruce, damp, mossy, darkly green, and pressed in on both sides. Ideal spruce grouse habitat. I was idly wondering how many of this rare and threatened species actually exist in the Park when three of the handsome birds crossed directly in front of my truck! They didn't scurry. No. They crept casually over the macadam, nibbling at tiny food items—insects, buds, needles—like tame barnyard chickens. This was a first.

I screeched to a stop, turned off the engine, and gaped. The male grouse had a bright red fold of skin above each eye which he distended provocatively from time to time. White bars crossed his black sides and his black chest and throat were neatly defined by a thin white line that set them off from the buffy brown body. His tail was tipped with a rich chestnut color. The two females were well-camouflaged in buffy brown with heavy barring.

The three "fool hens" paraded from shoulder to shoulder as I took careful note of the location. Their nickname is accurate. Spruce grouse are so unwary that they are easily shot, hit by cars, and taken by predators. A graduate student studying the birds once told me that during mating season males can act oblivious to anything except the hens. He once lured one onto his leg with a stuffed hen grouse. Yet so dense and difficult is their habitat that only a few hundred bird watchers have probably seen these forest recluses. The spruce grouse held me motionless for twelve minutes, and I considered it a gift.

Peddlers can have tough times and awful experiences, too. The detail work is burdensome. I must photocopy dozens of copies of my invoice form and scout out carbon paper for duplicates. Then I check the current prices on the back of each title. No editor ever advises me of a price change. If I don't catch it before distributing the books, I'll lose money and so will the shops. I jot each price on a sheet of paper and figure out the 40 percent wholesale discount prices. That will save time when making out invoices in the shops.

Arriving at a store, I take the order and make out the invoice. Then I climb into my truck, sort through cartons, stack up books, crawl out, carry them in, autograph each one, and hand them to the shop keeper. The invoice clearly says: *No Consignments, No Returns, 30 Days Net.* Some owners pay me at once. Some wait the prescribed 30 days. Others deliberately delay 90. Others conveniently forget—period.

Back home it's time to do boring bookkeeping. I have a large, black, hardcover notebook with a separate sheet for each store. All the sales for each title are posted, the amount owed, applicable shipping and

An Ol' Book Peddler

handling added. I have to update these at least four times a year. When owners fall behind in their payments, it means a special reminder letter. So embarrassing. At year's end I tally everything up.

I usually average between 1,200 and 1,500 copies sold. Please, dear reader, do not imagine there is a great profit in this. I buy my books at 40 percent wholesale, and I sell them at 40 percent wholesale. What's in it for me? My books have a life! Royalties come in a year later. The royalties on all titles *average* out at 84 cents per copy, not enough to live on by any means. Furthermore, readings and signings pay nothing to an itinerant author for her time and travel. Yet my books survive, and I do earn part of my living from them. That's exactly what I had in mind 20 years ago when I began free-lancing.

Book peddling also keeps me in shape. Consider the process. Books arrive from the publishers' warehouses in cardboard boxes weighing about 30 pounds each. I carry them from UPS truck to my truck, from truck to my boat, from boat to my cabin for storage. When it's time to distribute or mail out orders, the boxes go from cabin to my boat, from boat to my truck, and from my truck into the bookstore or to a post office. That's a total of seven carries! Yet I never feel sorry for having chosen this cumbersome task. It is my equivalent of Adirondack aerobics.

One of the worst spring trips I ever had was when I got *Giardia*, a waterborne parasite spread in human feces, while visiting Arizona. My symptoms were full-fledged by mid-May. Book distribution had to be done before Memorial Day. I'd lost several pounds and felt weak. It was touch and go if I could survive between shops without visiting a rest room. On one long, isolated stretch of road the cramps were so painful I had to pull off. Sprinting into the woods, I hid behind a large tree and kicked out a cat-hole with my boot, barely getting my trousers down in time.

Arriving at the next store, I was still trembling from the bout of diarrhea. The owner noticed my white face and clammy hands. She brought in a cup of hot tea laced with sugar and pulled out a chair for me. I'll never forget her kindness, and to this day I love to stop at this particular place and give this sweet woman a hug.

Later that day at Saranac Lake, I checked in at the local hospital's emergency room and begged them to do a lab test by microscope. Three hours later, my stool had been checked for parasites, I was diagnosed with *Giardia*, and I held a prescription for Furoxone (a much less debilitating drug than Flagyl) in my hand. Minutes later I swallowed the first pill. The irony of it is that I've never caught this parasite in the Adirondacks, where it's called "beaver fever" and is supposedly rampant. My three cases came from Arizona, Minnesota's Boundary Waters Canoe Area Wilderness, and Central America (where up to 50 percent of rural people harbor the little critter).

A far more sinister book-peddling adventure happened shortly after I became a Commissioner in the late '70s and was outspoken on some big environmental issues at the Adirondack Park Agency (APA). I had left my truck at a local gas station for servicing during the monthly meeting. I planned to begin book distribution right after the APA meeting adjourned, to take advantage of being in this part of the Park. After picking up my truck, I drove about 25 miles on a wooded highway without a stop till I came to the town of Tupper Lake. Slowing down for the first red light in all those miles, I pressed the brake pedal lightly, then harder, until the pedal touched the floor boards. No brakes!

Shifting down swiftly, I crawled through the intersection without hitting anything and managed to bump to a stop against the curb. Shaking, I locked the dogs in the cab and set off on foot to find a tow truck. By 6:00 P.M. the truck was fixed.

"What was wrong?" I asked.

An Ol' Book Peddler

The mechanic shook his head dubiously. "Don't know for sure, but something cut that brake line."

I paid, thanked him profusely, and drove away. How odd, I thought, that the problem occurred *after* driving 100 miles to the APA meeting, and *after* leaving it at that service station. The Agency was despised by some residents and appreciated by others. The same sentiments applied to its commissioners and staff. Could it be...? From then on, I refused to have my truck touched by anyone unless it was a trusted mechanic at a friendly facility. Better yet, I waited to have most mechanical work done outside the Park.

Over the years, I've seen many changes while peddling books. Our Adirondack roads have been improved. Some stores have expanded, others have gone broke. Publishers have shifted from those dreadful white plastic "peanuts" for packing to self-destructing corn starch ones that vanish in water. UPS and other shippers now offer overnight and two-day deliveries. I've learned to sign, pack, tape, and address a box of books in ten minutes. In order to accommodate all those dozens of cartons, out of necessity I bought an old farmhouse on a road, with electricity and space for storage. I work out of it during the worst of winter.

A group of fashionable businesswomen from an Ivy League college even called one day to invite me to lecture as a woman entrepreneur about my "boutique publishing business." I choked back a chuckle and said, "Well, I don't think I really qualify. You see all I am is an 'ol' book peddler.' Just because my corporation published two of my books doesn't exactly make me 'boutique.' I write for men as well as women. My main goal is to preserve Nature." Thanking them, I gracefully declined.

Two things, however, have not changed. I still schlepp every box of books seven times from its delivery to a bookstore. And I still earn less than the minimum hourly wage doing all this work because I'm my own employee. That's what happens when you're a capitalist, a for-profit corporation, and your own boss. Nevertheless, I like to do things my way. That's what it's like being an ol' book peddler—oops—I mean a "boutique publisher."

5

Condor

During this past decade at my cabin, I've been blessed with the company of Condor and his daughter, Chekika. (Xandor arrived later.) They became my protective escorts and faithful friends. Having two dogs made us a real "pack" and kept life energetic and colorful.

Condor fathered seven pups at age seven in Miami, while I was canoeing in the Everglades. Out of the resulting litter of three white males, three fawn females, and one black-and-tan, I chose the last. She would carry most of Condor's beautiful genes. This pup was considered the "runt"; yet since I'd chosen Condor as the runt of his litter, and he'd turned out so splendidly, I had high hopes for little Chekika.

He was a magnificent role model—full of wisdom, patience, and nobility. First and foremost, Condor showed the pup how to be a good guard dog, not only in the cabin, truck, and boat, and on lonely trails and waters, but in cacophonous cities and crowded classrooms. Chekika learned to bark and to mark her territory as confidently as any male dog.

The puppy didn't stay a runt long. She reached puberty at seven months and weighed 80 pounds by two years. She was extremely nimble and quick, dodging, feinting, pushing, leaping, catching snow balls and tennis balls in mid-air. I was never able to outwit or outperform her. She played constantly with Condor, who also took second place. I would say she lived up to her name, "Chekika,"—that bold, intelligent, strong, tawny chieftain of the Seminoles. He had fought to keep the Florida Keys and Everglades free from the white race in the 1800s. Chief Chekika was a Seminole hero and has a large park named for him west of Miami.

When Condor turned eight, he slowed down. The puppy showed no respect for his age and was devilish in her habit of leaping up to attack his ears. At first a mixture of Vick's Vaporub mixed with cayenne pepper smeared on these appendages protected him. But it didn't daunt her as a mature female with muscles like coiled springs. Condor suffered.

Those next two winters, my male dog aged rapidly. His legs became too weak to climb stairs or leap into the truck without help. He could barely follow us on afternoon rambles or cross-country ski trips. Deeply concerned, I had his hips X-rayed, only to find they were entirely free of dysplasia. That's one of the most devastating genetic disorders of shepherds and other large breeds. There was little arthritis showing on the films, and the veterinarian said, "Best hip bones I ever saw in an older dog."

She checked each of his four paws by bending them backwards against the floor and checking how he put them back into a standing position. They dragged across the floor. She checked Condor carefully for another few minutes and asked me to call back that afternoon.

When I learned of Condor's affliction I was near my cabin visiting a friend. It was a rare winter day when the land sparkled like diamonds, not a breath of wind, and the snow was blue-white as summer clouds. Balsams made elegant dark silhouettes against a blindingly blue sky. Yet in three minutes this brilliant Adirondack day turned from dazzle to darkness.

I'd borrowed my friend's phone to call the vet. "Degenerative myelopathy, or DM, is one of those terrible conditions that shepherds get," she began kindly. "It's like MS. No one knows what causes it. There's no cure. Condor won't be in pain. But he has CP deficits. The degeneration works from the tail up the spine," she explained. "Then it goes to the hind legs, next the front ones, and finally into the neck. Probably his tail doesn't wag now."

Condor, age eleven, with Anne on farm porch.

Condor gazes at the lake from cabin dock.

I clutched at my neighbor's wall to keep from falling. "No cure?" I whispered.

"Not yet," she replied gently. "But I've located some

literature that tells of a researcher in Gainesville. I'm going to write and see if there's a drug we can give to Condor to slow the progression."

"Oh, do! Please do!" I begged.

AMICAR. Aminocaproic acid. It is a large white pill used in humans who have bleeding disorders due to fibrinolysis, or who are hemophiliacs undergoing surgery. For an unknown reason, wrote the Florida vet, this drug seems to slow the migration of DM up dogs' spinal columns. He reported that 40 percent of the dogs treated with Amicar lived a year or two longer than expected. Of course, the earlier the disease was diagnosed and the younger the animal, the better the results. We decided to try it on Condor.

That medicine took a big bite out of my budget. It cost $150 to $160 per month. But I never counted the cost. Those words that I'd spoken to Brother Job, the monk in charge of breeding and training at New Skete Monastery, were still valid. I'd meant them when I'd bought the precocious puppy, and I meant them now that Condor was an innocent invalid.

"Having a dog is a lifetime commitment, a womb-to-tomb proposition."

Summer came and went. I gave Condor swims on hot days in my lake and various ponds. I held his torso in my arms and let his hind legs move freely. The trust he placed in me was implicit. If I had let go, he could have gone under and drowned because of lack of power in his limbs. I even wrote a poem about it, after one swim in a small pond.

SUMMER POND

The pond is summer perfect.
Alabaster thunderheads soar over in
churchlike processions.
Swallows swoop for insects above its tranquil surface,
Forming watered-silk reflections of the clouds.
Young birds twitter on slender branches,
Observing their parents' faithful gleaning,
As big bass patrol lazily among the
shimmering cattails.
Far off, soothing as a distant organ, the mowers hymn.
The farmers drive, toylike, sun-tanned, muscled,
Steadily harvesting July's lush grasses,
Each circle putting more hay into mangers for
plump cows,
Dozing under heat-slack trees and upon
fragrant wildflowers.
Surefooted and strong, I wade slowly into the
perfect pond.
The cool water rises up my back and arms,
Languidly it surrounds the dog I cradle,
Up, up to his chest, his neck, his chin.
He lies trustingly in my embrace,
Sighing contentedly as his heat subsides,
And I rock him tenderly over a cool spring hole.
His frail ribs are like latticework against my belly,
Backbone and hips as washboardy as a country road,
Droplets gleam on whiskers white as clouds,
Huge arthritic paws flutter helplessly at
wide-eyed bass.
Rheumy eyes peer startled at the pirouetting birds.
Too soon, too soon ....
The hay will be baled,
The swallows will be south,
The bass will be deep,
The pond will be ice,
My dog will be buried,
And the wildflowers
Withered on his grave.

When Condor's back legs failed, Anne supported him so he could swim.

The winter of 1990-91 passed slowly and cruelly. Since my dog had such trouble walking, we spent the entire winter at the old farmhouse I'd purchased recently. He never could have made it over the ice to the cabin. Condor lay quietly in resigned residence under the dining room table. From here he could see everything. His large brown eyes and black nose took in both doors of the farmhouse, the stairs, kitchen, office, and his food and water bowls. He could smell dinner being prepared and hear my truck come and go out back. I took him and Chekika strolling every afternoon. Sometimes he even tried to drag himself along our packed ski trails. Yet, his back end couldn't keep up with his front end. Then in January, his back legs stopped working—just like that!

Determined not to give up on him, I devised a dog hauler from a beach towel and a log carrier. Slinging them under his belly, I'd help him out to "do his business" four or five times a day. When it wasn't stormy, I'd leave him lying in the snow a few minutes so he could scent the air and connect with his surroundings.

Occasionally he was incontinent. Yet this seemed a minor inconvenience in order to keep him alive. I just kept laundering his sheet and blanket, hanging them to dry above the wood stove. I never considered how the dog might feel about it.

Condor could still travel around with me and Chekika by truck and on toboggan. When my secretary and I were working on the final draft of my new book, *The Wilderness World of Anne LaBastille*, we sometimes worked together at her office on a weekend. I had to be there to check pagination, lay out the proper place for photos and captions, and read for mistakes. She and I would place Condor on a blanket-draped toboggan and pull him over the snow to the front door. Then we'd slide him across the floor to a warm spot where he could watch us. We'd take occasional breaks during our formatting process to pull Condor outdoors for his "rest stop." These few moments of fresh air and bracing cold would refresh us for the next bout of intense work. So in his own way, Condor contributed to the production of my sixth book.

Sometimes I'd wonder when his front legs would give out. They were still powerful and helped to drag him forward; but if they failed, I knew he'd be impossible to handle alone. For the moment, however, we were managing. Even Chekika cooperated by not biting his ears and by keeping him company.

One afternoon I was carrying a load of firewood into the farm house. Stepping down the incline from woodpile to snowy yard, I fell with the heavy load in my arms. My left leg twisted underneath and sideways. I felt a ripping in my thigh. Lying dismayed on the cold ground, I tried to assess the damage. I felt a gap or dent across the middle of my thigh and could feel the muscles contracting on either side of it. With a chill, I realized I had maybe an hour before pain and immobility set in. I must stand up, move firewood indoors, take Condor out briefly, feed both dogs, get something for my own supper, plus pain pills, and locate my old crutches in the truck. I still kept for emergencies the aluminum pair I'd used after I'd fallen in the woods and broken my pelvis years back. The harsh winter night was coming on and snow was predicted. No way I could drive to Lake Placid and see a doctor.

The pain was still minimal, but swelling had begun as blood poured out of torn blood vessels into the injured area. I forced myself to manage all the chores and prepare a makeshift bed next to Condor and Chekika on the floor.

A sports medicine book described a tear to the body's largest and most powerful muscle—the quadriceps. Mine sounded like a grade III tear, which warned of great tenderness, muscle spasms and swelling. The book prescribed RICE (rest, ice, compression, and elevation), also, the use of crutches. That night was horrible. By morning I couldn't walk.

But Condor *had* to go out. Experimenting with the crutches, I gained my balance, then studied how to manage the dog in his carrier. Two crutches were impossible. I could only do it with one crutch on the side of the injured leg and the opposite arm holding up Condor. That maneuver took about 15 minutes to travel 25 feet. Our world was reduced to moving that distance four times a day, or 200 feet every 16 hours.

A few days later I braved the drive to Lake Placid where a doctor wrapped my thigh in a much wider, stronger bandage. Then things were easier. Yet I had to be very careful not to fall and rip more muscles, nor to drop the dog. The frustration, fear, pain, and demands of the problem affected all three of us.

One frigid February night, I dragged Condor out, let him pee, and left him in a snow bank. Chekika wandered off to inspect her territory. I stared at the gorgeous, implacable stars and suddenly started screaming at the inky black sky. No one could hear me, so I screeched and raged at God, at myself for failing my beloved dog, at the callousness of Nature. I fixed tear-swollen eyes on the North Star and tried to imagine the millions of people and animals—wounded soldiers, arrow-shot deer, women dying in childbirth, car accident victims bleeding to death, road-killed wildlife, battered wives, beaten mules and children—who had stared at that star and hoped for help and relief. Without response...

I thought about giving up and leaving Condor in the snow. At 20° below zero he'd simply freeze to death, the way old Eskimos do when they decide their lives have run out. But I couldn't do it. I stopped raging, looked down and hugged my dog. I saw Condor was shivering violently and looking forlornly at me. How much time had passed in that paroxysm of grief I'll never know. I struggled to get us both inside again. The dogs and I were *very* cold when we finally settled down by the wood stove.

More than a month had passed since Condor stopped walking. He ate less and less. He still was taking Amicar, plus buffered aspirins when I perceived he might be in pain. Then one morning he wouldn't eat at all and seemed very weak. I rushed him to the vet. She found he was bleeding internally, apparently as a result of all the medicines. She put him on IVs and gave him a blood transfusion. When she had him lying comfortably in a pen, she took me aside.

"It's time to let him go, Anne," she said softly. "Condor doesn't want to live like this...peeing in his bed, seeing your frustration, sensing he'll never walk again. Would you? I don't even know if I can cure his bleeding stomach. Honor his dignity. Let him go." I shook my head. "No, no," I moaned. "He may get better. I can't live without him." She answered crisply, "It's not you we have to think about. It's Condor." I stumbled out and went home. Chekika and I sat close to each other for a long time. The vet's honest words tumbled through my mind. Was I being selfish? When is too much love a bad thing? Should Condor be put to sleep?

Considering my own philosophy on death, he should. I strongly believe that each human has the right to end her/his life if it gets too difficult, painful, or is terminal anyway. My many legal papers make this crystal clear—a Living Will, a medical power of attorney, my last will and testament, and the wishes I've shared with close friends. This woodswoman never wants to be kept alive by heroic or artificial means. I believe in a compassionate, careful, doctor-assisted euthanasia for people. So why couldn't I practice this kindness on my dog?

Next day Condor had not improved much, although his stomach bleeding had stopped. I sat in his pen all afternoon and coaxed him to eat a small piece of chicken. Hope flickered as he nibbled and swallowed. I smoothed his fur and stroked his head as I considered one of the hardest decisions of my life.

That night, a Sunday, I called Mike, my former doctor love. We had not been able to sustain our relationship and had parted some time ago. Both of us were too devoted to our work—he to saving patients, me to saving the environment. Each felt shortchanged by the other's ever-present demands. Yet we still kept in touch. Now I needed him desperately.

After hearing of Condor's medical symptoms, Mike agreed with the vet. "Put him to sleep, Anne. It's the decent thing to do."

"Let me wait one more day in case he improves," I temporized. "If not, I'll do it Tuesday morning. Will you come and be with me? Please?"

A long pause followed. Mike was fighting with his own set of values—helping to save life whenever possible versus helping to kill the dog he'd given me and

Condor

loved, too. Finally he murmured, "I'll be at your place by 9:00 A.M. and then we can drive over to the vet's. What will you do with the body?"

That had been planned last summer when I was at the cabin. Steeling my nerves, I'd dug a grave for Condor next to Pitzi. It had to be prepared before the ground froze and the lake turned to ice. The hole was covered with plywood. There was no way my pet would end up in an incinerator, or mass grave, or whatever happens to most dog and cat corpses. He would come home with me to rest beneath the balsams and pines.

Monday he was the same. I spent hours with him, registering every move, every twitch of his eyelids, every small sign. The dog hadn't eaten since that scrap of chicken. He slept a lot. That afternoon I faced the vet and said, "Let's put him to sleep tomorrow morning. But I want to be sure he doesn't feel a thing. I want you to give him a tranquilizer beforehand and let me hold him in my arms throughout the process."

She nodded bleakly. "That's fine."

Mike came as promised, and we drove to the animal hospital. He stayed outside, smoking a cigarette, while I went in. Approaching the pen, I hoped above hope that Condor had rallied overnight. Instead, when I slipped into the pen and called his name, he simply opened his sunken eyes. I lifted his head and he growled. It was the first time in his 12 years that my dog had put me on notice. That told me more than any human advice that *he* was ready to go. Mike refused to come in. The vet administered the tranquilizer with a tiny syringe. Condor never stirred. Only his breathing slowed.

She came back with a much larger hypodermic filled with a strong narcotic. Squeezing my shoulder, she said, "He'll feel no pain. His heart will just stop from shock. He'll be dead in less than a minute."

I braced myself against the back of the pen and encircled Condor with my arms. It was the last minutes of his life, and the last time I'd feel his warm body, broad buffy chest, thick fur and big ears next to me. After the shot, I broke down sobbing. So did the vet and half the staff.

Eventually we carried Condor to the truck and called to Mike to open the tailgate. We laid the dog on blankets heaped upon a red plastic toboggan. Mike whispered, "Goodbye, old-timer".

"You okay?" he asked me gruffly.

Suddenly I realized how ill-prepared he was for this. "Yes," I replied steadily. "I'll drive Condor to the cabin now."

"I need to get back to my office," he explained apologetically.

"I know."

"Well...have a good trip, Anne."

Then he was gone. I started crying again, as much for him and our lost love as for Condor. Sometimes even the strongest men have their weak moments.

Nearing the lake, I stopped to find Andy, my good friend. He'd offered to go up to the cabin with me and bury the dog. Quietly, we lifted out the toboggan with Condor on it. He looked so peaceful. Andy and I put on warm parkas and fastened our snowshoes. Then I tied a long rope to the sled and started pulling.

The day was another frosty, flashy, blue-white extravaganza. Better this than a gray, dismal, snow-spitting one, I thought. When I tired pulling our sad burden, Andy took over. We barely talked. When we reached the cabin, I unlocked it and turned on the propane gas. Fixing two large, hot cups of tea laced with sugar, we rested for a few moments, sipped, and warmed ourselves. Then I found a snow shovel and we cleared off the gravesite. Andy dragged the plywood to one side.

As I'd done with Pitzi, we wrapped Condor in an old wool red-and-black jacket. His food and water dishes, collar, leash, and a red bandanna were ready to accompany him. I said a short prayer before we lowered him onto the balsam boughs at the bottom. I managed not to cry.

Andy saw the problem immediately. The pile of dirt beside the grave was rock hard and could not be used to cover his body.

"Bears!" I gasped to my friend. "If they find this grave open when they emerge from hibernation, hungry and mean, they'll *eat* Condor!"

Sensing my dismay, Andy started rummaging in the woodshed and came back with a stout black tarp, several chunks of firewood, and another piece of plywood. "We'll cover him with this tarp so odors can't escape, then shovel snow on top to keep him frozen as long as possible. Then, I'll lay the wood over the snow, plus more plywood and cement blocks. When you come home in spring, Condor will still be frozen. Don't worry."

Through the whole process, Chekika sat puzzled on the snow, watching every move. I talked to her soothingly and let her sniff her father and look down into the grave. I kept murmuring to her until everything was covered over and it was time to go. She had to learn to deal with Condor's death, same as me.

Andy was right. In late April, when I returned to camp, nothing had disturbed the grave. But Chekika and I had entered a period of extended mourning for Condor. I found it hard to work, to write, to think. Often I stared into space by day, cried by night. She lay still, head on her paws, watching me for hours. "Where's my daddy?" she seemed to be asking.

There's no way to hurry grief. It just hangs over your heart week after week like a miasma. The thought of a new puppy was repulsive. But now that I was home at my cabin and the ice and snow were gone, I sensed it was time to put this emotion behind us.

Before Memorial Day I sent a formal note to Condor's best friends, inviting them to come pay their respects to this noble dog. "Visit any time during the last week of May."

I got busy edging the grave with balsam logs. Next I hauled away the plastic tarp, logs, and plywood. The dog was as hard as granite underneath. In my boat I brought up pails of small pretty stones of pink, white, and gray found alongside our dirt road. With these I covered the bare earth. They matched a tiny tombstone that my dear friend, Doris, had ordered. It simply said: CONDOR. Last, I planted periwinkle vines and one little balsam on the plot.

Each evening I lit three votive candles and set them atop the stone. Chekika and I would sit near the grave at sunset for a few minutes. Somehow being beside it was reassuring, stabilizing. When I awoke in the night, I could look out the window of my loft and see the candles glowing. Slowly I recognized how these rituals sooth and push the progression of grief.

The first person to arrive was Doris. She was en-

A granite tombstone adorns Condor's grave. His friends brought purple flowers, an amethyst, and white pine tree (at side) as memorials.

route to a conference and only had a few moments to spare. She placed a huge purple flowering plant next to the stone she'd given me. Whispering a short prayer to Condor and crossing herself, she took me in her arms and we both sobbed.

A longtime camping buddy stopped to console me on his way to Oregon. He brought steaks and baking potatoes, built up a big campfire, listened to my story, even made me laugh. He, too, had a message for Condor.

A new friend, a sensitive masseuse, came next day. Maya immediately told me she sensed Condor's soul nearby. Reaching into her daypack, she brought out an amethyst geode of palest lavender. She set it gently beside the tombstone. "Amethyst attracts light and good vibrations," she explained. "It will make Condor's passing smoother." The crystallized quartz twinkled in the sunlight.

Before leaving, Maya massaged the tension from my rigid neck and shoulders. "Try to open your mind to the presence of Condor's soul," she counseled. "It will console you."

Finally Brother Job drove up from New York City. Only now he wasn't a monk. Returning to secular life, he was considered one of the best dog trainers and dog authors in the country. Job Evans lavished me with gifts. There was a specially signed copy of his latest book, *People, Pooches, and Problems,* the sequel to the acclaimed *How to be Your Dog's Best Friend.* Next he laid a Ralph Lauren package on my lap. I opened it to find a cashmere-soft, brown wool blanket.

"It's brown because that's your color," he said. "Brown for the woods. Brown for your cabin. And brown like your eyes."

Most importantly, Job conducted a small, nondenominational service for Condor. He spoke to the departed dog, reminiscing about his roots back in Germany. Of the farm where his ancestors had herded sheep; and where all were buried. The names of his grand-, and great grand-, and so on. One was an earlier Condor on the pedigree. Then Job praised him for being such a good pet to me.

"You were my favorite puppy of all those litters at New Skete—ever. I honor your passing, Condor."

The woods were very quiet around us. I fought back my tears. Job cleared his throat several times. He knelt and planted a small white pine in front of the tombstone. My balsam stood to the left. Incredibly, I could visualize my dog right there, hovering around us, between the trees. The feeling was in my heart and chest, as palpable as the fullness one feels when first in love.

I can't explain it scientifically. Remnant electrical charges? Energy waves still emanating from his body? Some sort of telepathic vibration? All I know is I sensed this life force in the same way when I first hugged the giant white pine near my cabin.

Job's sweetest gift was helping me to see that dogs, like people, have souls. They shimmer around us like sunbeams and moonlight—*if* we care to believe.

6

The Lake That Loves Loons

It was my third day swimming without the loons. Usually I started my July days with a dawn dip, sculling silently to within 100 feet of the majestic pair. This encounter always filled me with energy and appreciation. How many other bird watchers can boast of a similar wilderness wakening?

Now I began thinking that something may have happened to Nina and Verplanck.* I thought back to the last few boat trips I'd taken between my cabin and the road two miles away. A single skittish loon had hugged the shore. I'd also seen the usual occasional osprey, two great blue herons, a pair of hooded mergansers, and many tame mallards, which the summer folk insist on feeding. They were all accounted for. I thought back to the past several nights spent camping outdoors. Loon tremolos and yodels had definitely drifted in and out of my sleep. Clearly, Nina and Verplanck were still somewhere on Black Bear Lake. Why were they avoiding me?

How lucky I and my summer neighbors are to live in this six-million-acre Adirondack Park—the second oldest-and-largest park in the continental United States. It is about 40 percent state-owned with "forever wild" forest and great tracts of wilderness, and about 60 percent

---

*Named for the visionary creator of the Adirondack Park, Verplanck Colvin.

private lands. At least 150 pairs of loons survive and reproduce here on *some* of the 3,000 lakes and ponds. Many other states have had to declare the common loon a threatened or endangered species. Yet New York still considers populations to be at healthy levels, though decreasing in numbers. Every year, however, more lakes are spoiled by acid rain and shoreline development, and in danger from increased large motorboat and personal water craft ("jet ski") uses. Thus, the loon population bears careful monitoring, and it is labeled a "species of special concern" in our state.

More mornings passed without seeing my swimming pals. Much too late for the pair to have eggs or chicks, I thought; otherwise, I'd suspect they were quietly incubating. I began to worry.

That noon was a scorcher. Temperatures rarely rise much over 80°F in the Adirondack Mountains—let alone 90°F! But this July they did. The woods were silent except for the monotonous monologue of a red-eyed vireo. I sunbathed on my dock, gazing drowsily over the green forested hills, the calm blue water, and the cluster of grey granite rocks at my point. A few barn swallows dipped and dove over the lake. The tall grass on the islet across the bay shimmered and shook in an odd way. But I was too hot to be curious.

A short time later a yellow canoe with two paddlers pushed off from the island, skirted the bay, and stopped at my dock. The two strangers said they were exploring and had enjoyed a picnic on the little island. (That explained the movement of the grass.) He was muscular, tall, and flushed. She was a pretty petite blond with tousled hair. Shortly after they paddled away a distraught neighbor, Linda, whizzed up in her motorboat. "Anne, Anne," she shouted. "You've got to help. The loons are in trouble! Those people on the island, they almost rolled over a loon nest and two eggs!"

The Lake That Loves Loons

"Two eggs?" I exclaimed. "But it's so late in the season. Nina and Verplanck have never nested here before either. Remember the artificial nest platform the Fish and Game Society set up in the inlet? The loons ignored it completely for five years. Are you *sure*?"

"Yes, they *have* got a nest now and they may desert it due to all that commotion," Linda claimed indignantly.

"They were just having a picnic," I inserted innocently.

"Picnic! Picnic!" She fumed. "It was a rather intimate luncheon, if you ask me."

"Oh!" I said, my mind racing. "Here's what we'll do then. You go back over right away and put up a sign that says: CAUTION — STAY OFF ISLAND — NESTING LOONS. I've got plywood and paint if you need them."

"Sure," Linda said excitedly. "and how about a couple of signs down at the public dock and parking areas? That will let outsiders know, plus any property owners who do not belong to the society."

"Right," I agreed. "But we mustn't say where the nest is, so as to protect the birds and eggs. You know how some people would do anything to grab a photo of a loon."

"There's another thing we can do," I continued. "If you and your daughters could come over tomorrow morning, we could mail out requests for help to all members of the Fish and Game Society."

"Good thing we're organized on this lake," she nodded. "We'll need to cooperate. I think we also should ask the cottage owners right around this bay and the islet to watch. We can be vigilante guards."

Thus began the great loon security drive at Black Bear Lake. Word spread. Signs went up. My immediate neighbors and I watched the nest site like falcons. If anyone came too close, a vigilante would rush out, politely explaining the situation. We used no force, no bribery, no rudeness. Our sole weapon was to say,

"Look how lucky we are. Loons are rare and beautiful. This is the first time they've had eggs here. Let's all help them hatch the chicks, fledge them, and fly away."

Our strategy worked. Very soon the loons became parents. During my dawn dip I saw both of them floating near the islet, each with a tiny bump on their backs. The chicks were off the nest. Time for me to worry again. Loons look for a secluded nursery site as soon as their chicks hatch. The babies spend less than 24 to 48 hours on the nest before moving to this critically important new habitat. It must be peaceful, free of people and boats, and offer cover such as snags, rocks, driftwood, and low-hanging branches where young can hide. Black Bear Lake has practically none of these conditions in a backwater area. Since there's no road, owners access their private property by motorboat and canoe all summer. It's not at all like Stillwater Reservoir, which has the largest breeding population of loons in the Adirondacks. The shoreline of that huge body of water is mostly state land, with points, coves, islands, bays, and plenty of driftwood that give 14 pairs of loons ideal nursery sites.

Nevertheless Nina and Verplanck managed. They picked a shallow cove edged by birches and firs. The one existing small cabin was owned by Linda and her family. They, of all people, would protect the loon family.

Soon the parents started showing Rocky and Henry (named for Nelson Rockefeller and Henry Hudson) how to fish, dive, escape danger and scout around the lake. It became clear that the Society had done several favors for loons and other fish-eating birds and mammals. About 15 years ago, when we first learned of acid rain and found our lake had a pH of 4.5, we decided to combat it. Decisions were made *not* to lime the water due to negative side effects and cost. Instead, the Fish and Game Society asked the New York State Department of Environmental Conservation to stock the lake with acid-resistant strains of brook trout. Every autumn since then a fish hatchery truck brings 5,000 fingerlings up the rough dirt road to the dock and dumps them in. While some fishermen grumble at sharing their potential catches with loons, most of us are overjoyed to still be able to feed them (especially at the expense of the state). Moreover, loons also eat bullheads, leeches, perch, frogs, and aquatic insects, therefore little competition exists for trout fishermen.

In addition, years ago we began to notice a decrease in water quality as the lake community grew. A water sampling and testing program was started. Shockingly, one summer our "pristine" body of water showed fecal *E. coli* counts of up to 2,400 bacteria per 100 ml in some spots. (*Escherichia coli* is a bacterial indicator of pollution levels from feces of warm-blooded animals.) Safe drinking water should have counts of zero to ten bacteria per 100 ml. This caused grave concern among cottage owners since many of us drink lake water and everyone swims. I'd been dipping my buckets of drinking water from the lake for years and had never been sick. Indeed, "wild water" seemed to agree with me. I wasn't about to stop.

A Pollution Control Committee was formed, on which I volunteered. Every cottage and cabin was dye-tested. The septic systems were checked for breaks, leaks, or insufficient leach fields. Any small problems were fixed for free by the committee. Big plumbing problems were the responsibility of the property owner. Two years later, the fecal *E. coli* count was 2. Our water was once again eminently drinkable. The water quality has stayed that way. This grass roots conservation work also helped the loons. These birds usually inhabit crystal-clear lakes ringed with wild, old-growth forests. They will not tolerate unclean waters. So thanks to the lake's voluntary pollution committee, our loon chicks had a healthy home.

The Fish and Game Society had accomplished still

another measure of protection for lake and loons. This was a Water Craft Resolution, passed by a large popular vote, that prohibited "jet skis" and hovercraft; limited outboard motors to less than 50 HP and posted hours for waterskiing. This community resolution helped keep our lake fairly quiet. It reduced the large wakes that were eroding our shorelines, rocking our docks, swamping loon nests, and chilling the eggs (a major cause of chick mortality). It also helped ensure water safety of canoeists, sailors, guide boaters, swimmers, *and* baby loons.

Nevertheless, now a few weekend skiers were reluctant to slow down or reduce their hours just for a couple of loons. "Stop skiing this afternoon? Are you loony?" One of them asked a vigilante guard sarcastically. All we could do was hope the adult birds had figured out the skiing schedule and routes and kept their chicks close to shore.

Late night boaters were another concern. In New York, bars stay open until 2 A.M.; movie theaters until midnight. Obviously, there were no restrictions on when people boated home. It was summer and vacation time. Nina and Verplanck, nonetheless, were *very* upset by late evening traffic. Every boat that traveled after dark brought forth torrents of cries, shrieks, and moans. Evidently, the loons perceived danger from dark boats on the dark lake. I had occasional nightmares of high speed boats with whirling props slicing a poor chick into bloody chum. Some loon-lovers talked to those habitual night owls and urged them to carry bright lights and stay in the center of the lake.

In retrospect, knowing that water carries sound vibrations better than air, I'm sure the loons could hear and avoid speeding boats by day. I'm not sure about them by night. Each fuzzy brown chick had to learn to escape danger by traveling stealthily behind one parent to cross the lake. It moved by short swims and tiny dives. Only its head would emerge like a little cork. On calm evenings I sometimes heard a soft "*cuck*" sound from an adult as if coaxing its baby to stay close.

Oddly enough, it was probably a raccoon that killed Rocky close to shore. At 2:00 A.M. one night a terrible racket resounded over the lake. Next day Linda reported seeing only one chick. The mail boat driver passed the word around cottage owners. Many people searched carefully, but only one chick was observed from then on.

Labor Day came and went. Summer vacationers left for home and school. Every night I could hear the chirps of migrating birds above my dock. A few diehard woodswomen and woodsmen stayed on. Canada geese began to migrate, winging crisply across the stainless blue sky. Glorious autumn reds, maroons, oranges, and golds swathed the hills. My dawn dips shortened and stopped, yet still the loons passed close by as I splashed chilly water on my face. Henry was always in tow, brown and fluffy. He was two-thirds the size of his parents. By now most Adirondack loons had flocked up and were ready to head south. Once a strange loon settled on Black Bear Lake, causing great displays and vocalizations among Nina, Verplanck, and the visitor.

I counted the days until first ice—October 7 to maybe November 15—only 38. When would Henry's flight feathers come in? Why didn't he flap his wings? When would he start to fly? Would he know how? Could he figure out when to leave? Or where to go?

One October morning as mist rolled over the still lake and the tamaracks reflected golden in the rising sun, I realized Verplanck was gone. Nina and her son floated tranquilly near the islet. Their black silhouettes were almost the same size. Suddenly I felt more hopeful.

That night another strange loon put down to rest. Nina gave a bizarre repertoire of wing-beating, shrieks, furious paddling. Henry disappeared. What *if*, oh, what

if, I thought, Nina is seduced to leave with another male? Yet she stayed. Now I noted Henry flapping his wings occasionally. What mysterious lessons was that faithful mother giving him? The fish hatchery truck arrived and dumped 5,000 trout fingerlings in Black Bear Lake. Good! Plenty of "fast food" to strengthen Henry's muscles and courage.
Hunting season began October 23. I checked to see that the loon signs were still up. It wouldn't do if a hunter got drunk and tried some target practice on Henry. Fortunately, common loons are covered by the Federal Migratory Bird Treaty Act. They are protected from taking, harming, harassing, pursuing, hunting, wounding, buying, selling, and possession. This includes adult birds, eggs, chicks, and nests.
The nights chilled down. Ice edged the bays. On November 2, Election Day, my boat froze to the dock. I chopped a channel with my axe so I could get out and vote. "Where's Henry?" I wailed, looking everywhere for the youngster. "Please don't be frozen in the ice!" Two days later, a spell of Indian summer opened the lake completely. There sat Nina and Henry as if it were summer. Yet November is a most treacherous month. I carried an axe and big laundry bag constantly in my boat in case I found the fledgling in an icy prison and needed to rescue him.
By November 12, I knew from past experience that it was time to go or risk being stuck at my cabin for three weeks during freezeup. I ferried boxes of books, cameras, and files to my truck. No sign of Nina. No sign of Henry. On the final morning, with temperatures hovering about 33°F and the hills as grey as a beaver's belly, I tearfully locked up my cabin. I waved goodbye to the tiny flock of chickadees and nuthatches in the firs. Out on the lake nothing moved upon the mirror-like, pewter-colored water. Somehow I knew that little Henry and his Mom were on their way to meet Verplanck. Maybe they'd rendezvous on Chesapeake

Bay, maybe near the coastal islands of Georgia, or even off Key West. There'd be plenty of dangers and challenges during their long migration. Yet I also knew instinctively they'd be back at Black Bear Lake next year. Teenage Henry will be flapping his wings and preening over by the islet while Nina and Verplanck send sweet duets over the sparkling water.

7

Twister

The heat wave that hit the Adirondacks in mid-July 1995 was practically unprecedented. Day after day the thermometer reached the high 80s and even low 90s. The smell of hot pine pitch, spruce gum, and balsam resin wafted medicinally through the forest. The lake had warmed to 79°F and snorkeling became a pleasure. We were fortunate compared to people in the mid-West. There it flamed to over 100 degrees for days, and the death toll in Chicago was frightening.

One night I tossed uneasily in my lean-to where it was cooler, clad only in "T"-shirt and panties. Chekika and Xandor, my new shepherd, panted. At 2:00 A.M. I almost got up, thinking of heading back to the cabin to work at my desk. But I convinced myself sleep was more important. The radio hadn't mentioned any thunderstorms or cold fronts. Besides, it didn't feel like that kind of weather. It was dry, tight, penetrating heat.

Around 4:00 A.M. I dozed off. Suddenly the noise of an enormous ship coming up the lake jolted me awake. My watch said 4:55 A.M. The dogs were looking out of the lean-to. Before I could even stand up, a blast of wind slammed into the shoreline and a giant fist thudded against my shelter. Rain slashed horizontally. Lightning flashed nonstop above the hills. Deafening waves of thunderstorms rolled rapidly out of the southwest, crashing above the lake.

Swiftly, I slid back the screen doors of the lean-to and

Twister

yelled at the dogs, "Come on, boys, we better dash for the cabin."

They hung back. At that instant, a huge snag fell behind us. Flying limbs could be heard ripping through the forest. If we ventured out of this small shelter, all three of us might be hit. I realized we *had* to stay put. I also realized we were in a tornado!

I tried to think what people did out in Oklahoma. Something about hiding in the basement, or standing in the doorway of a small room in order to have more support around you. Nothing like that here. My lean-to was flimsy. It was built simply of Adirondack siding, a few upright spruce poles, and a metal roof. No place to ride out 70 mile per hour winds with downdrafts up to 100 MPH and lightning flashes of one per second!

Turning back inside, I searched panic-stricken for a spot in which to hide. The rain had drenched me. The dogs were soaked. My pillows and sheet were sodden. Another big snag thumped to the ground a foot and a half from the lean-to. Both dogs lay down prostrate at the rear of the structure, their noses pressed into a corner. They had picked the best place, even as they trembled from heads to tails.

I threw myself on top of Chekika and Xandor to protect their bodies and pulled the wet mattress over us. If a tree or big branch poked through the roof, it might keep us from being impaled. The last thing I noticed before the mattress shut out the view was an ominous, evil, green light spreading over the sky. Then I started shaking uncontrollably and my teeth chattered like castanets at this display of Nature's raw power.

The onslaught worsened and lasted 15 minutes. It was the most terrible storm I'd ever been in. Even that perilous boat crossing from Nassau to Miami with my husband and our friend, Bruce, in *Snowbird*, years ago, ranked a second.*

---

*from *The Wilderness World of Anne LaBastille*, 1992, "Maiden Flight of the Snowbird."

As quickly as it had come, the tornado—actually a very broad front of powerful microbursts called a *derecho*,—moved eastwards. The green light faded. At 5:20 A.M. the dogs and I got up. Our trembling eased. Instinct told me it was safe to move back to the cabin.

"Before we look at anything, boys," I announced shakily, "we're going to make espresso, fix your breakfasts, take a dip just like any other dawn, and get dressed."

We scampered down to the cabin. I noticed five small trees across the trail. Any one of them might have injured a dog or crushed my skull. Without looking left or right, I performed the daily rituals. They calmed me. Then I steeled myself to discover the damages. First I closed all the windows and mopped my desk and chair dry. I flicked on the battery-powered radio and tried to find the usual stations. Blank. Radio towers or power lines were probably wiped out. Finally I picked up the strong Kingston, Canada, station and heard that a severe line of thunderstorms and windbursts had roared through southern Ontario before dawn. It had continued on in a line between Watertown and Utica (more than 100 miles wide). There was damage in both cities, but most of the *derecho's* force occurred on forest preserve lands.

Then I tried calling a neighbor across the lake. His sleepy voice answered after several rings. "Are you all right?" I asked.

"What do you mean, Anne? Geez, it's only six A.M. You woke me up."

Incredulous, I blurted, "The tornado! The twister! The thunder and lightning! Didn't you hear it? Don't you have trees down around your camp?"

"Hang on," Hank said. A minute later he came back on the line. "Nothing that I can see."

I filled him in on the radio report. "The storm came out of the southwest," I reasoned, "so maybe your side of the lake was in the lee. I'm going to call next door. Bye."

This call was far different. Sara and her little girl were home alone this weekend, as her husband had gone away on a business trip. Sara was wide awake, audibly shaken, and afraid to move. She asked me what to do.

"Make any calls you have to real fast," I ordered. "The lines will probably go dead soon. Don't let your daughter or the cat out until you've had a chance to trace the electric lines. They may be lying on the ground and still hot. You don't want any person or an animal to step on them by mistake and get electrocuted."

She shuddered audibly over the phone.

"As soon as it's lighter outside," I continued, "bring in buckets of water, candles, lanterns, flashlights, and canned food, and have firewood ready. You may be cooking on a campfire and flushing by hand for quite awhile. Your power's off, isn't it?"

"Yes," she mumbled.

"I'll call back, but right now I want to get hold of the town police, health center, and forest ranger. Also, we should try calling anyone on the lake who may need help. Some of our older neighbors, or those in poor health, don't you agree?"

News from the authorities was tragic. A professor and his family camping at a local campground had been struck by a large tree. It had flattened their tent, killed the man instantly, and wounded his wife. In the northwestern part of the Adirondack Park campers and hikers were boxed in, stranded, and tangled within several massive blowdowns. Seven hundred miles of trails were damaged, as were several state campsites. Cars and trucks had been crushed. House roofs were dented or torn off completely. Dozens of people had been injured, and first aid was being given by EMTs on site. Many roads were closed with dozens of trees across them. Surely our dirt road was impassable.

Overall, the damages from *this* blowdown were not

as widespread nor as bad as those of the 1950 blowdown. An estimated 100,000 acres had half of all the trees blown down. The storm 45 years before covered a far greater area. However, one important fact made this one worse. No one was warned that these microbursts were coming. They were spawned swiftly by very hot air moving over the still-cool Great Lakes. The resulting turbulence churned up, down, and around, then pushed east rapidly, smashing into the northwestern slope of the Adirondack Mountains. In 1950, the tropical hurricane which moved up the coast and caused such devastation in the northeast had been predicted for days. Then, everyone was prepared and had things secured.

Surprise! At 10:30 A.M. the mail boat made its rounds. The roads had been chainsawed clear so the mail truck was running. Did the federal government have clout? Or what? Within five hours of one of the worst storms of the century, mail was being delivered.

After making my phone calls and meeting the mail boat, I inspected my property. This was only the second time in my life that I'd experienced the incredible power and total implacability of Nature, along with the most abject terror and vulnerability humans are capable of feeling.

Directly in front of my cabin a big balsam had snapped in two and the top had crashed onto the main roof. It sliced off the 16-foot CB whip antenna, then slid down on top of the tiny roof that covers my propane tanks. The weight of that very bushy crown could have snapped the stems off six large propane tanks and turned the place into a rocket launch site and holocaust.

Walking around the corner of the log building, dogs skulking behind, I beheld a swath of flattened trees, 200 feet wide and extending as far back as I could see. Big maples 20 inches in diameter, tall balsams, saplings, spire-like spruces lay in a matchstick mess.

Some had snapped in half or corkscrewed down, but most were uprooted. The former understory of woods grass, hobblebush, and emerald ferns was pocked by black root-holes filled with water and rocks. My "backyard" looked like a moonscape.

At the woodshed, the roof was littered with big branches. The water tank cover was bent crazily. The trail to the outhouse was completely obliterated by two huge balsam tops. Otherwise the outhouse was fine. The lean-to where we had cowered had a huge snag lying two inches from the rear wall; another, 18 inches from the side.

My favorite big white pine—the one I learned to hug and draw energy from—was still standing. It had a slight tilt to its arrowy trunk, and it was a lone sentinel now, flanked by its fallen fellows. In total, just within my main outdoor living and working space, perhaps two acres, I counted 33 trees down. All of them pointed northeast. Apparently my point of land had split the tornado in half. One massive windburst had whirled into my land and headed northeast, while the other had moved southeast to strike my neighbor's property and take down 34 trees!

Thoreau II, my special writing retreat and sanctuary, would have to wait to be checked another day...*if* I could even get there.

Back inside my log cabin, I sat down and tried to sort out what had happened and collect my senses. I drew Chekika and Xandor close to me and cuddled them. We were alive! We had been lucky! We had a warm, tight, undamaged home with gas appliances. Everyone else on the lake faced thawing freezers and frigs, no water pumps, no lights, no TVs, no electric toothbrushes or coffee makers, whereas I could function as normally as I'd been doing for years on gas, wood and candles.

The dogs stopped trembling and fell asleep. I told myself sternly that we had to go on with life. The trees could be cut up, even if it took three years. The wood could be split for firewood. Brush could be burned, trails cleared. I could manage all the minor repairs alone. Would this be any different than putting your life back together after a car wreck?

Ah, but it was. I felt a tremendous sense of betrayal. I felt dazed and bewildered and depressed. A car wreck was caused by human error and bad judgment. It could be avoided. But this storm...No way. My main love and strength in life—Nature—had turned on me. She had almost killed me. She had wreaked havoc with my carefully tended and protected woodlands. She had scared the hell out of me, Chekika, and Xandor. She had shown herself unmanageable. Could I ever trust Nature again?

In reasonable ecological terms, this *derecho* and blowdown were not new events in the forest. Such storms are natural incidents that happen sporadically over time. They actually can be good for old-growth forests by opening up areas and allowing new species and young trees to spring up in sunny clearings. There will be other microbursts over the centuries. But I hoped never to see one again.

Nature began making amends within the first hour after the storm. The birds began to sing again! How could they, I wondered? How could they go through the same ghastly event as I had, having no warning, and still *sing*?

An hour after my inspection of damages, I was moodily brushing my teeth at the kitchen window. Glancing out towards the lake, I could see no evidence of the microburst. Most of the damage lay behind the cabin. My eyes fell on the elk antlers which hang from the log wall right under the window. There, on the highest point, sat a princeling ruby-throated hummingbird, glittering in the sun. He was looking back at me, as pert and cheery as any bird could be.

Amazingly he had made it through 70 MPH winds

and drenching rains. Where was he sleeping when the great wind roared through the forest? A creature weighing less than a quarter could have been tossed upwards, flung hundreds of yards horizontally, and slammed back to earth like a piece of flotsam in a tsunami. Had he hidden his body in the crotch of a branch? Crept into a crevice of bark? Did he have time to scuttle to the lee side of his tree? Did he ride out the twister in that curious torpor into which hummingbirds fall at night? Their body temperatures drop several degrees and the birds are as sluggish as black bears in March. Or did he leap into the wind and hover at peak power, muscles burning at 133 watts per kilogram (as compared to 1.5 watts per kilogram for a human marathon runner), and ride out the storm like a minuscule space ship?

I would never know the answers to all these questions. The one thing I was sure of was that the hummingbird felt the same overpowering terror that Chekika, Xandor, and I did. The tiny, audacious male whirred away with a flash of crimson gorget. He and five females buzzed around the feeders more actively than I'd ever seen. At times, three would be sipping at the three holes on the same feeder at once. Maybe that was the way to handle the twister, I thought. *Get busy. Eat.* Abruptly, I put down my toothbrush and began making more sugar water for the hummers. Then I brewed another espresso and toast. My healing process started with the hummingbird...

My recovery was not steady, however. I couldn't bear to sleep in my lean-to. Nightmares woke me up. Chekika and Xandor whimpered often in their dreams. Every day brought some awful new spin-off from the twister.

Two days after the storm I found a dead myrtle warbler on the ground. It was crushed grotesquely. I cradled the tiny scrap of brown and yellow in my palm. How many more warblers, woodpeckers, orioles, robins, and owls lay dead in the forest? Gently, I buried the warbler next to Condor's grave.

Four days later I began noticing a sweet, cloying, perfume-like smell in the air near the large, downed maples. No flowers were blooming nearby. I couldn't figure it out. Meanwhile, the leaves of those maples were starting to curl and fade as the sap flow from the massive root structures dwindled to nothing. Gradually it dawned on me that the sugar content of those dying leaves was probably fermenting under the hot sun. It reminded me in part of maple syrup being boiled down in a sugar house, and in part of the faint smell that subtly creeps from old people before they die. My mother had a strange, sweetish odor three days before her death. Never before had I smelled a large vigorous tree die. It lasted for weeks, giving me an overwhelming feeling of sadness.

A week after the tornado, power had still not been restored to our community. In order of priority, villages were fixed first, then main roads and hamlets, and finally, the outlying lakes and remote cottages. Linemen were working 16 to 20 hours a day. Crews and equipment had been brought in from other states. But the damages were so extensive that they predicted a week to ten days until lights would burn again at Black Bear Lake.

My neighbors' nerves were frayed thin. Two or three local women called up, whimpering and complaining. "I can't stand another day of hauling pails of water to the toilet. How do you manage it, Anne?" And, "I can't use my computer, and my kids are acting wild without cartoons and Nintendo." Plus, "Everything's rotten in my frig; we're living on peanut butter and boiling our coffee on a campfire."

"Why don't you go back home to the city until things are fixed?" I suggested as kindly as possible.

"But, but—it's our *vacation*," each one blurted out.

"If you're hating it so much, then it's not a vacation," I reminded them. "Look at this like a great adventure."

Secretly, I wondered how their great-grandparents had managed. Or how they imagined people in the Third World lived, and what those people were eating.

That night I was asleep in my cabin when a boat suddenly stopped at my dock. Someone ran up to the door and called my name. The dogs barked wildly. Grabbing my flashlight, I hurried to the entrance and recognized my next-door neighbor.

"Anne, I've got a man down in my boat. He was walking along your shoreline. I saw his flashlight when I stepped down to the dock before bed. You have any idea who it could be?"

"A man on my shoreline?" I mumbled groggily. "What time is it?"

"Eleven-thirty."

A prickle of fear ran up my back. "I can't imagine who'd do a thing like that. Did he give you his name?" I asked.

"Ted, or Tom, or...I can't remember. He seems suspicious. Look, I'll bring him up the path. Don't let him in. Maybe you'll recognize the guy. Keep your dogs inside."

"Okay," I agreed, "but wait a minute while I go back in and get my pistol. Just in case!"

I ran back out with my .25 caliber Colt in hand and, with the safety on, and confronted the stranger.

He was scruffy, disheveled, and dark haired with a sweat-band, the beginnings of a dark beard, a lump on his forehead, and sunken eyes. I didn't know him at all.

Keeping my distance, pistol in view, I asked politely what he was doing walking around on private land at night. He eyed me cautiously and said, "I'm with the power company. Our crew was brought in from 200 miles away. I'm checking the lines." My neighbor and I glanced at each other skeptically.

"Well, maybe so, but we have reason to be nervous," I began. "There are so many..."

My neighbor interrupted, demanding to see some identification. The man fumbled through his wallet, handing card after card to my friend.

"Won't do, won't do," he snapped, getting more edgy.

Finally, the man produced his last card. "Here, Electric Federation. That's who I work for."

My neighbor glared at it under the flashlight, then said, "Okay, you're okay." He handed it back without showing it to me.

I lowered the pistol, thinking that the company should certainly give their linemen caps, badges, name tags, or arm patches to show the public.

"Put your gun away," begged the man. "Please, it makes me real nervous."

"Fine," I agreed, "but I want you to understand that I live alone, need some form of protection, have a valid pistol permit, and have taken rifle and pistol training. I'm not threatening you."

He looked at me blankly, stuffed his cards back in his wallet, and turned to my neighbor. "Would you mind taking me down to the public landing. The rest of my crew is probably there along with the trucks. I'm terribly tired. Been working 18 hours straight. Can hardly keep my eyes open."

After they left I was still so edgy and upset that I barely slept. Yet I had a big job planned for next day. My good friend Andy was coming to cut up the first of the fallen trees. He'd been Rodney's assistant on many a trail crew and was expert with a chain saw. I was busy at dawn, getting our gear ready. As I approached the dock, I noticed he was deep in conversation with a man in an Electric Federation van. Andy turned to tie up my boat and said, "Anne, this is one of the foremen from the power company."

The man jumped out of his van and we shook

hands. He was smiling, and his blue eyes held a twinkle. "I, ah, came up here, ah, to speak to you," he began. "One of our crew reported a woman confronted him with a gun last night. Rumors are flying around. Could you, ah, tell me about the, ah, incident?"

I explained the whole scene in detail. Then I added, "How come your employees don't wear identifying clothing or caps or badges like meter readers do?"

"We really should do that," he replied. "But these poor guys have been working nonstop all week. Some haven't been home to change clothes. They're sleeping in their work clothes most nights. I'm sorry you were scared. I know you'd never hurt a fly. I've read your books."

"If you like," I offered, "I'll write a letter to your supervisors, explain everything, and send a letter of apology to the lineman."

"Great idea," said the foreman. He jotted his name on a piece of paper and handed it to me. "Send me a copy, okay?"

We shook hands again and he drove away.

Andy and I headed up the lake. As soon as we got around the point, he gave me a wicked little grin. "You're a pistol-packing Mama again!" he quipped. "Just like you told in your first book when those tipsy hunters yelled at you across the lake at night. I heard all about this 'incident' at six A.M. when I went for coffee."

I let out a guffaw. "How do rumors..."I began.

Andy laughed and said, "I know, I know. The incident happened at midnight. But the rumor mill works 24 hours a day up here. Apparently the lineman told his buddies."

"Aren't you afraid to work with me?" I teased. And we both broke out laughing.

That evening just before dusk another boat came by and someone let out a long high whistle. I ran to the dock with my dogs as two linemen cruised up.

"We'd like permission to use your dock and trail back to the power lines that go around the lake. The worst breaks are behind your camp and your neighbor's next door."

"Of course," I answered pleasantly. "Let me show you the way back there."

The two men jumped onto the dock. I let the dogs sniff them over. One fellow was about six-foot five and as burly as a big yellow birch. The other was about six feet, well-muscled, and trim. They began to follow me, carrying ropes and other gear.

"I'm the one you talked to last night," the shorter man announced hesitantly. "Ted."

"*You* are?" I stuttered in amazement. "But, but—the man last night was dark, had a beard, a sweatband, and looked...oh, I don't mean to insult you."

"That's all right," he said, with the suspicion of a smile. "You seemed quite upset last night, being woken up and all. Yet that *was* me. Maybe it was too dark to really see. I finally had time for a shave, shower, and change of clothes today."

This man looked distinguished. His hair was grey and neatly cut. His face was tanned. I stopped staring and continued on the trail. The two linemen quietly followed, their wide leather belts creaking and their tools clanking as they walked.

After a couple of minutes I turned to Ted, who was right behind me and said, as sincerely as possible, "I'm so sorry I scared you last night."

"Well, I didn't appreciate the gun," he replied frankly.

I looked him squarely in the eyes. "Honestly, Ted, you were in no danger at all. The safety was on. The dogs were inside. I'd never shoot anything unless it or they attacked me. *That's* self-defense."

He nodded.

"I'm really a gentle person," I murmured, so only he could hear.

"So am I," he said softly.

I gave him a startled glance, not used to a man admitting such a thing. He was looking right at me. His eyes were blue, clear, and kind. We both smiled. Suddenly the night's fear was forgotten. Stumbling a bit on the trail, I faced forward, but not before my heart had also taken a little lurch.

At the power line, I said, "Come and go as you need to, and use my dock for your boats. If you work real late and want coffee, wake me up and I'll be glad to fix you some."

"We've got plenty of work cut out for us," said the burly lineman. "Just look at how those poles are tilted and the lines touching the ground." He walked confidently up to one and grabbed it in his rubber-gloved hand.

I gave a gasp. The dogs pricked up their ears. "How do you know it's not hot?" I asked. "You could be electrocuted."

With an easy grin, he said simply, "We know."

Ted pulled on his own rubber-insulated gauntlets and they strode away down the right-of-way. I returned to my cabin and gathered up the dry sleeping bag, pad, and pillows. That night I would sleep in my lean-to for the first time since the twister. It seemed like a peaceful place again. Purple finches were warbling an evening song from the spruce tops. Far off a hermit thrush sang harmonics of liquid notes. Big bull frogs bonked along the shore. If the linemen used their boats or my trail, I never heard them. That sleep was the second step of my healing.

The big trucks were parked at the public landing for three more days. Linemen hung the lines and reset the poles. Their shouts filled the woods, but I never saw them to speak to. If we passed on the road, we waved. No one seemed upset with me. My letter went out to Electric Federation supervisors, with copies to the foreman and Ted. In it I praised the crews for their backbreaking, risky work, referred lightly to the "incident," and suggested some sort of permanent identification in the future. Power was restored and our community settled down. At least for a couple of days—until a major fuse on the line blew.

All at once the men were back, retracing the right-of-way by night, yelling to one another like little boys in dark spooky woods. Next morning, I had to go to town for a dentist appointment. As I was unlocking my truck at the public landing, Ted drove up in one of the big rigs.

"Hi, there," I called, happy to see him. "Seems like our lake is a trouble spot for you. How're you doing?"

"Great!" he said, leaning out of the cab window. "Say, I was looking for you today. I have something to give you." He reached over on the seat, raised his hand, and pointed a pearl-handled small gun at me!

My heart almost stopped. A wave of fear paralyzed me. Could he be bent on revenge? Did he mean to shoot me? Had I been wrong about that kind look in his eyes?

A jet of water hit the truck door just below my open window. Ted chuckled. "I wanted to shoot you with my water pistol."

Summer zoomed by. It was hot, very hot. A few friends came to visit and helped me cut up trees. The terror of the tornado slowly eased. I spent many busy days clearing and burning fallen branches. Sometimes thoughts of Ted and his quirky humor drifted through my mind.

That fall another, smaller wind storm zipped through the Adirondacks. But this one was localized and far less powerful than the July 15th event. It dropped trees that had been weakened and tilted by the big twister. Andy lost nine trees in five minutes in his yard. Again our electric lines took a few blows, and the linemen came back. This time my neighbor, Hank, across the lake—the one who'd slept through the tornado—was hit. He

Twister

came to use my phone and report the lines down. While Hank was chatting, a heavily laden boat with four linemen came to my dock. They clanked up the path to my cabin and called out, "Hey, Woodswoman, you got some hot coffee for us?"

They crowded into the small studio lined with books and furs. All of them managed to find seats, and they looked around appreciatively. Ted was there. So was the big burly fellow, and a woman lineman. The cabin glowed with energy, jokes, and laughter. I dithered back and forth to the kitchen, fixing tiny cups of espresso and passing around doughnuts. I felt a sense of camaraderie and warmth. The pistol incident seemed years ago and all but forgotten. Things sometimes have a way of leveling out, I thought.

I smiled at Ted. Yes, his eyes *were* blue, clear and kind; yet, also shy. He smiled back, raised his hand, and sipped his coffee. A wide gold wedding band glinted on his hand. I hadn't noticed it before. In fact, he'd worn no rings at all when I saw him pull on gauntlets. It was probably too dangerous, working in the woods. I sensed he was subconsciously telling me something. Something that he'd been thinking about over summer.

Without that ring, I realized we might have liked to know each other better. But with it, there was no way. It was, after all, only an "incident."

8

Guiding

*Come join the wilderness world
of Anne LaBastille
in the Adirondack Park of New York,
where a dawn dip with loons
starts your day...
where campfire readings
are more heart-warming
than cellular phone calls...
and where the hoot of a barred owl
or chorus of coyotes
is more valid than a TV or radio.*

This is how the front page of my new brochure for West of the Wind Guiding Service read when I reactivated my guiding business. I'd almost given it up over the previous five years, for many reasons.

For one thing, the New York State Department of Environmental Conservation requirements had tightened. An old-fashioned one-page reference from a local game warden and a two-dollar fee no longer sufficed. There was an exam to pass. Each guide picked categories of expertise and paid a fee for each. Mine were camping, canoeing, hiking, and natural history instruction. My annual fees came to about $75. A guide needed Red Cross courses in water safety, first aid, and CPR, renewed every year, with cards to prove it.

A guide also needed a physician's statement of

Guiding

good health and fitness. Most important, one had to have insurance. Ours is a litigious society. A guide would be crazy not to have liability coverage. Recreating outdoors can be perilous. Clients fall out of boats and drown. Canoes can capsize. A hiker may break a leg on rocky trails. Someone may get sick back in the woods and blame the guide. Five years ago the only policy available cost over $2,000. It would have taken a summer of guiding just to pay the premium. Then new insurance companies formed and rates went down. When I found a million-dollar policy that covered my motorboat, canoes, gear, and clients for about $700, I felt ready to start guiding again.

I re-enrolled in the New York State Outdoor Guides Association and placed an ad in their *Guide to the Guides*. This private group is very helpful in promoting ethical guiding, advertising, and networking. Finally I made up my new brochure and waited to see what would happen.

Several inquiries came in from professional women and small family groups. My first clients were a doctor from Chicago and a professional public radio fundraiser from New York. I thought we'd make a great trio. A week before our trip, I called both women to answer questions, set up our meeting place, and explain my guiding philosophy. "I don't like to kill anything," I said, "be it fish, fowl, or furry animal. Rather, I want to instill a love for all wildlife and respect for Nature. We can do this through trail talks and campfire readings of wilderness literature."

"Sounds good to me," said Dr. Young in Chicago. "By the way, how hot is it there?"

"About 90 degrees this evening," I told her. "Very unusual for these mountains. It barely cools down to 80 at night."

"Well, it's 104 degrees Fahrenheit in Chicago right now," stated Dr. Young. "Our clinic is closed. Everyone's been told to go home, stay quiet, and use fans or air conditioning. The death toll is already 300!"

"When is that heat mass supposed to move east?" I asked anxiously. "Won't be any fun to hike if it's that hot *next* week."

"The radio said two or three more days like this," she said.

After covering a few more details, we said goodbye.

By the time the two women arrived, of course, that heat wave had broken—snapped by the violent microburst front. Cool unsettled weather followed.

I was still wrestling with my fear of tornadoes and my depression over the damages. Yet I had to put on a brave front and act cheerful because both women were complete novices to camping, canoeing, and the wilderness. They were probably scared about everything, I thought. It was my job to reassure, protect, and instruct them.

They drove separate cars to Black Bear Lake, arriving about 4:00 P.M. I invited them to my cabin for coffee and cake. Dr. Young and Mrs. Bernhard jumped into my outboard boat like good sports even though a summer thunderstorm was rumbling down upon us.

"We can make it safely to my dock," I assured them, glancing back at the ominous clouds.

"How can you tell?" asked the doctor nervously.

"By watching where the lightning strikes and how long before the thunder answers," I replied. "Also by the way the wind blows."

True to my word, we arrived at the cabin dry and unscathed. There was enough time to make a quick outside tour. My clients were surprised by a lean-to with sliding screen doors and an outhouse with a framed poem, dry posies, and zero odor. They felt dismayed by the blowdown and deep black root holes. Both were enchanted with my colorful cabin and extensive library; astonished by propane gas lights and old rotary phone.

"This is where I called you from during the heat wave in Chicago," I explained to Dr. Young. "And this is the desk I wrote you on," I said to Mrs. Bernhard. "Essentially everything's the same as when I built the place. Of course I've had to replace the old frig and woodstove, but the only new item is my phone. I have to have one to speak to editors, set up lectures, make air reservations, and order my books. But I wish I didn't!"

Slipping into my tiny kitchen to fix espresso and cut pieces of peach cake, I let them browse over the furs, knickknacks, and books, and consider life in a log cabin without electricity. During coffee we quickly got on a first-name basis—Tina and Donna. The former was short, slender and dark; the latter, tall, willowy and blond. Both exuded intelligence and energy. Carefully, we went over our lists of gear and the medical kit. We had to make sure nothing was forgotten for our week-long sojourn in the woods. I showed them our life jackets and stressed they must be worn whenever on the water. We examined the tents, tarps, my pretty blue enamel cookware and dishes, the coolers, blue-and-white checked tablecloth, and box of freeze-dried foods. Everything was neatly packed in blue plastic crates and looked ship-shape.

"I never realized how much equipment we'd need for this trip," exclaimed Tina.

"Yes," I replied. "Say, I'd love some help in loading it and the canoe on top of the truck tomorrow morning. How early can you get back here in the morning?"

We agreed on 8:00 A.M. in the parking lot. They arrived on time, brimming with excitement. After loading everything, we drove to a large wild lake with a boat launch site. Within two hours we had the motorboat launched and loaded, the canoe trailing behind, the dogs leashed inside, and my truck and trailer parked. Both women slathered sunblock over their pale skins and put on sunglasses and hats. Watching that ritual, I wondered about living a life without sun, wind, and open skies every day. I knew I couldn't stand to be cooped up in an office or hospital.

We soon stopped for a picnic on a long, clean, sandy point. We munched sandwiches and threw sticks to the dogs in the water. I said, "After lunch, you'll get to pick out your very own campsite."

"You mean you don't know where to go?" exclaimed Tina, with a frown.

I chuckled. "Sure I do, but I want *you* to like your tent site. It'll be your home for five and a half days. Do you want a point, a woodland setting, a view, a beach? Would you rather face east for the moonrise, west for the sunset, or south for the sun? Will you feel safer near that boat launch and the forest ranger's station or way up the lake where you'll scarcely see any people or boats? Our only guideline is to tent 150 feet back from the water."

"Stop, stop!" laughed Donna. "I had no idea camping involved so many choices. It's not like booking a motel room exactly. Where would *you* like to go?"

"As far away from noise and habitation as possible. Maybe on an island. One of the delights is waking at dawn and wading right into the lake and swimming near loons."

They clapped their hands in unison like kids. "Let's go find that special place!"

Toward 5:00 P.M. we picked a small island that was off the main section of lake and very peaceful. I had decided to always ask each client to be personally responsible for setting up her own tent, maintaining one set of dishes and silverware, and helping bring in firewood and water. How else would they learn to camp and feel comfortable with wilderness living?

So I handed each woman a new tent and said, "Try putting this up yourself. Instructions are inside the carrying bags. I'll help you if you need me."

Before dusk we were nicely set up. The three tents were pitched on the wooded, north-facing shore, which would be shady and cool. The east side of the island held a sloping sand beach. A loon pair floated right offshore. West lay a marsh and the mainland, a great place to see deer, bald eagles, waterfowl, and great blue herons.

While the women were working, I'd set my tent discreetly off to one side under a leaning maple so that Tina and Donna could feel more private. A guide treads a fine edge between being a servant, i.e., running motorboats, hauling gas, cooking and boiling water, washing dishes—and being a friend, teacher, counselor, and first-aid provider. I never want to intrude, so I make it a rule to announce at the start: "If you wish to be left alone, need silent time, or don't feel like talking, take this special red bandanna and tie it around your neck. That means, 'Please give me some privacy.' Otherwise, the bandanna stays tied on our shovel. When one of us goes into the woods to pee or poop, she takes the shovel to dig a cat-hole *and* the bandanna. The others notice the bandanna is gone and respect her privacy."

For supper I'd brought a thick steak, big baking potatoes to put on the coals, a ready-made salad, and the peach cake. This was an easy meal. As days went by and the coolers no longer held ice, it took more imagination to prepare food. We'd resort to peanut butter sandwiches, canned salmon, instant rice, and peaches in syrup.

Tina approached me shyly. "I have to go to the bathroom. Where shall I do it?"

Beckoning to her and Donna, I grabbed the shovel and led them back into dense woods. Soon I saw an open space on the ground and began digging. "The reason we dig a cat-hole," I said, jumping vigorously up and down on the shovel blade, "is to protect the lake where we'll be swimming, getting our drinking water, canoeing, and watching wildlife. Also we want to keep flies away from our campsite because they can carry germs."

"You know better than I, Tina," I panted, "how sewage can leach through the soil to contaminate water, and how certain flies can transmit disease."

She nodded affirmatively.

"As long as you dig your cat-hole 100 to 150 feet from *any* water body, there's no problem."

I handed the shovel to Donna. "Give it a try. Jump hard. Remove the duff and dirt down about six to twelve inches. Do your business and fill the hole. Pick a different spot each time. The t.p. will disintegrate underground."

Donna was trying, but the shovel barely made a dent.

"Harder," I insisted. "Jump harder."

"I'm trying," she groaned, "but I never used a shovel before."

Tina watched as the hole slowly deepened, then said, "How do you keep from falling in?"

"Just watch how Chekika pees," I grinned. "She puts a hind paw to each side and squats. That's it. You won't fall in."

I left the two women busily digging a couple of holes and ran back to turn the potatoes beside the fire. Donna surprised us at supper by opening a small cooler and producing a chilled bottle of white wine and a six-pack of imported beer.

"Help yourselves," she beamed.

Our dinner was delicious, the setting perfect. The driftwood fire sang and sparked. Loons yodeled half way across the still water. Distant hills turned the color of faded blue jeans. Long shadows stretched across the bay from gigantic pines. Peach, mauve, and raspberry wisps of clouds streamed overhead. We reclined on the warm sand. The only sound was the scrape of forks on enameled plates. Both dogs were sound asleep, their bellies full and muscles tired from chasing sticks.

"When's the last time you could *not* hear a gas engine of some sort?" I queried softly.

Tina and Donna looked at me in astonishment. "Why, why, never," stuttered Donna. "Manhattan's never quiet."

"Once when I was little," Tina said, "my parents took me to northern Michigan on vacation. It was so *still* up there. I don't remember another time. This silence sounds weird."

No one spoke—listening—really listening—to the silence. I noticed both women had relaxed considerably from this morning. They sat propped lazily against driftwood snags, sipping the last of the wine. They made a striking pair: Tina with long, flowing, raven-black hair and Donna with short, curly blond ringlets; Tina with stern spectacles and Donna with zany red earrings; Tina with tiny feet and Donna with large hands. Fine women, I thought. The trip is going to be good.

Donna stretched, sighed contentedly, and asked, "How did you get into guiding, Anne? Seems quite unusual for a woman."

I thought back over the years and answered, "I guess it all began with Rob, an older guide and neighbor. We used to go hiking once a week and explore a new lake each time. Saw at least 50. He vouched for me on my first guide's license. It was quite unusual then. Now there are dozens of women guides out of an estimated 2,000 licensed in New York State. Later, Rodney, my best friend and a master guide, taught me more. Sometimes it was how to use a special old-time tool or a clever technique in the woods. I sure miss them both since they've passed on."

"I'll bet they would like to be here now with us," murmured Donna.

"They are," I said simply. "After Rod died, I carried a bronze plaque way back to a huge white pine that Rodney loved. It's attached to the trunk and reads:

Rodney R. Ainsworth
Gentle Woodsman...Our Friend
March 14, 1905–June 3, 1989

His soul is right here in the woods with us."

The women were silent, listening intently. Then I added, "It doesn't get much better than this. We have a super site. There are no bugs. Weather's fine. We have plenty of dry firewood and pure water. Chekika and Xandor are here to protect us. Don't you worry about bears. Just the dogs' odor will send them scooting."

"I imagine this is how the earth used to be all the time," mused Tina. "No planes, no trains, no atom bombs, no TV." She yawned.

Guiding can be hilarious. Here, Xandor tries on Anne's guide hat with badges.

Guiding

"Bed time," I said. "It's been a long day. Call me if you need anything. Good night."

Next morning when I slipped out of my tent, the red bandanna was missing from the shovel handle. Perplexed, I wrapped myself in a large towel and walked to the beach. Donna was sitting on a driftwood log, writing. The bandanna was spread next to her.

I waved briefly and picked a place to swim where I would not disturb her. The loon pair was preening nearby. I gave a soft loon call to calm them as I waded in. They moved off and floated motionless, watching this odd, tousled, silver-blond ball approach. Since I sculled underwater with my hands, the birds heard nothing. I came within 75 feet of them. When I emerged dripping, Donna motioned me over.

"I write in my journal every morning," she explained. "It takes about an hour and is a form of stress therapy. Dreams, thoughts, feelings. My job is very demanding and this helps."

"Yes, it must," I said.

"Say, is there any coffee?" she asked.

"Sure will be in five minutes. Let's make a pact, Donna. The first thing I'll do each morning," I promised, "is make espresso and bring you a cup. I'll say `Good morning!' and go swimming. You *write*."

After breakfast, the two women decided they'd like to hike. We chose a beautiful wilderness lake that lay a mile north of this large water body. It was accessible by a pleasant level trail; however, I explained that we might run into serious blowdown. "This area of the Park was hardest hit by the microbursts. Some gusts reached 100 miles per hour and whole hillsides were flattened. The forest ranger told me they had to evacuate hikers by helicopter because many trails were obliterated."

"We may be lucky though," I added. "A trail crew has been in here for a week, trying to open up the lake trail. Hopefully we'll make it."

As we meandered along a bubbling brook, Tina began giggling. "I just remembered the dream I had last night. You made me dig a cat-hole seven feet deep and seven feet wide to pee in. But it was so huge that I fell in and couldn't get out. I guess it really was a nightmare."

We laughed so hard we had to stop walking. "Are you a little anxious, Doctor?" I joked. "Or what? Sounds like you miss your flush toilet."

We passed a narrow stillwater, black as obsidian, where graceful old cedars curved from the banks. A cold spring seeped down into the pond. I bent down at once and scooped up water for a drink.

"You're sure it's safe?" asked Tina. "I can't believe we can drink water that's not been chlorinated."

"Would I allow us to get sick?" I countered. "I'd have to cart you out to a clinic 30 miles away. This spring is probably the purest water next to distilled. I'll bet my pal Rodney took many a cool drink from it when he

Stretching out on the abandoned Adirondack Division tracks, Anne sniffs wildflowers as she waits for the train.

worked on these trails."

We hit some blowdown, but by walking single file through sections sawed out of huge fallen trees and climbing over rotted snags we made it to the lake. It lay nestled in a cleft of forested hills, tranquil, clear and calm. Puffy clouds were reflected on its surface. A pair of loons floated here, too. The far shore showed no evidence of twisters uprooting any trees. However, the eastern shore and trail were blocked. We couldn't hike any farther.

A sad sight met our eyes. An old lean-to with half a century of names and graffiti carved on the logs had burned down. Only a few rusted spikes remained scattered about the four foundation piles of rocks.

"What happened?" asked Donna, appalled.

"Careless campers," I guessed. "They probably stayed here several days, kept a campfire going, then failed to douse it properly. It's been so dry this summer that the coals burned into the duff, fire traveled underground, and it popped up underneath the lean-to. You can imagine how tindery those old logs were, plus the tar paper roof. It's a total disaster!"

"I feel sorry for the men who walked way back here and spent their time building this lean-to," said Donna. "Gosh, there's no electricity or anything. It was all hand labor and hard work."

Sobered, we hiked back out and returned to our island in time for an afternoon swim. Two days passed pleasantly. Tina and Donna learned to canoe, identify trees, went fishing, sunbathed on wild beaches, scouted for driftwood, and even tried hugging virgin white pines.

"I don't feel anything," wailed Tina, her short arms trying to clasp a 24-inch diameter trunk. "In your book it sounded so easy to tune into the energy of a big tree and feel part of Nature."

"It takes a few tries," I explained. "You have to stand very still, put all thoughts out of your mind, look up at the branches, and think like a pine. You keep hugging. I'll leave you alone for a while."

"Don't go too far away," she begged.

That evening before dark I read from *Walden* as they lay on the sand, cuddling Chekika and Xandor. Thunderheads sailed along the horizon, but overhead the sky was milky blue. The air was muggy and warm.

"It may rain tonight," I predicted mildly at supper.

"Oh, Anne," pleaded Tina. "Why don't you move your tent closer to ours?"

"Sounds like a good idea."

Before dark we dragged in more firewood and draped a blue tarp over it, weighted down with stones. I strung another one between two trees and fashioned a slanted roof. Underneath I placed the life jackets, axe,

Silhouetted by dawn light, Tina enjoys a solitary paddle as Chekika watches.

coolers, dog dishes, plastic bottles for spring water, and some extra kindling.

"Let's each collect one more handful of kindling in case this bunch gets wet. We'll squirrel it away in our tents, between the rain flies and tent walls."

I showed them how to break off squaw wood (dead twigs low down on evergreens), where to find dry grasses and ferns, what bark burns well (birch curls from yellow birches), and to pick up dry pine cones. "This little bundle of kindling means the difference between a hot bowl of oatmeal and a smile on your face, or bread, cold water, and a drenched jacket in the morning. You've always got to think ahead of Mother Nature."

I slept lightly. When a clap of distant thunder resounded at 2:00 A.M., I unzipped my tent, piled more wood on the fire, rechecked the boat anchor, and woke up the women.

"Sorry to wake you," I said softly. "Don't be afraid. A storm's coming, so you should check your tent stakes, go pee, and get your rain gear handy. Here are two big golf umbrellas so you can walk around and not get wet."

Tina scurried out, wild-eyed, and opened her umbrella. Donna followed, calmer. "Come with us into the woods, Anne," they both begged. "It's so dark back there."

When they crawled back into their tents, I comforted each one, reminding them that summer T-storms are normal. We were not near any tall trees which might attract lightening, nor under any "widow-makers" (dead branches that could fall). Also our tents were new and well sealed at the seams, so they should stay dry. Then a blinding flash of lightning sent me and the dogs scuttling into our shelter. Chekika and Xandor began trembling, and, to tell the truth, so did I. This storm was so near in time to the twister that I had an instant gut reaction.

The rain sluiced down for two hours. The dogs and I lay close together and shuddered. I tried to think what would happen if those torrents leaked into the tents and soaked the women. They'd probably break off the trip next morning. At the first lull, I crept out and opened my big umbrella. Donna and Tina were wide awake, exhilarated, and dry. Not a drop had entered the three tents!

That thunderstorm cemented our relationship. It made Donna and Tina more courageous and self-confident as campers. And it was the third step in *my* healing process.

The rain also left a gift. The slanted tarp had sagged in the middle and caught several gallons of crystal water. "Good!" I crowed. "I won't have to boil lake water for you to be safe. We can fill our empty plastic bottles right here."

"Is this safe to drink?" queried Tina, always on the watch for stray bacteria and parasites. "What about acid rain?"

"It's probably as pure as that little spring we found by the trail," I replied. "The acidity of rain won't hurt you. It's the heavy metals and ash from burning fossil fuels which might be hazardous if drunk day after day. But after that deluge last night, I'm sure this rain water is quite clean."

Donna celebrated by washing her hair in a bucket of rain water and declared it had never felt so soft and springy. Better than any New York City beauty shop treatment!

Quietly, to myself, I compared their urban lives to mine and thought about how far removed humans have gotten from natural living. Were all city folk suspicious of springs and rain water? Did they always fear bears and storms? Why were they so preoccupied about bathroom facilities? Could they ever survive without electricity and flush toilets? Both conveniences masked the problems of waste disposal and energy demands in an ever-more crowded world. True, they had ways of surviving in Manhattan and Chicago that I could never imagine. I'd be as scared of living *there* as they were of going into the woods alone. It all pointed to the amazing adaptability of humans. The message to me is that one needs to have skills in both worlds today. Sooner or later most people have to enter a city, if even for a day. And we never know when people may be forced back into the country to a simpler way of life.

That evening was our last. Since the sun had come out and dried our island, we lay again on warm sand in front of a roaring fire.

"What did you like best of the whole trip?" I asked.

"The storm!" announced Donna at once.

"Drinking from that spring. It was such good-tasting water. And not getting hurt or sick," said Tina thoughtfully. "And the soft, green, mossy trails."

"What did you like least?"

The two women looked at each other self-consciously.

"Digging those darn cat-holes," they admitted, "and going into the woods three or four times a day."

"Well, at least you didn't pollute the water like the raw sewage outfalls from New York City do!" I retorted.

"How about you?" they asked, turning curious, suntanned faces toward me.

"As always, swimming with loons and sipping espresso on a beach," I replied. "On the other hand, that storm really shook me. It sounded so much like the tornado. I was glad you were here."

Donna and Tina stared at me nonplussed. "You mean *you* were scared?"

"Sure," I answered. "It showed me again that Nature can be uncontrolled and chaotic. Yet now I see that she has limits. I must learn to handle her bad sides without getting panicked or personalizing the experience. You have to trust yourself to come through okay."

Next morning the camp was abustle. Packs, bags,

coolers, tents, cans, and axe were being piled back in the boat. The canoe was tethered behind. Blue tarps, ground cloths, and life jackets were stacked on the beach. The dogs barked and jumped.

"I'd like to be back at my car by 3:00 P.M.," said Donna. "That way I can be home in the city by 9:00 P.M."

"Me, too," agreed Tina. "My flight's not till tomorrow, but I want to visit friends on the way to Albany."

Suddenly we were back in the fast track—schedules to meet, planes to catch, miles to go. The tranquil glow of the past few days diminished. Finally our campsite was vacant except for the left-over stack of firewood and ring of stones.

Tina started to climb into the boat.

"Before we leave, let's move the wood and stones

Anne and small family group prepare hot dogs at a wilderness lake.
Photo by: Robert L. Stevenson

Guiding

into the woods so it looks untouched by human hands," I said. "We'll leave it as we found it—pure wilderness."

Both women looked at me appraisingly, but came to help. When we finished, they started to get into the boat again.

"One more thing," I entreated. "Please just give me five more minutes of your time."

They came back to the beach reluctantly. I explained, "I'd like to make a sweep across the ground we camped on and look for any scrap of paper, matchstick, bobby pin, or candy wrapper...anything artificial we might have dropped by mistake. You'll be surprised at what we'll find. Imagine how little stuff could pile up year after year, if each group of campers fails to clean up meticulously."

Sure enough we found a wire tie-on, one of Donna's red earrings, the wine cork, and a book of matches.

"Now come to the fire site and hold hands," I instructed. "It's time to say thanks to Mother Earth."

"First, Mother Earth," I began, "thank you for keeping us safe and giving us your ground to sleep on, warm sand to lie on, trees to shade us, and your water to bathe in."

I picked up a spare cook pot, went to the lake's edge and filled it. Slowly I poured water over the blackened ashes. "Second, thank you, Fire, for cooking our food, boiling our water, lighting up the night, keeping us warm, and protecting us." I handed the pot to Donna and motioned for her to do the same. She did. Then Tina followed suit.

"And last," I murmured, squeezing the hands I was holding on each side, "I want to thank you both for coming to the Adirondacks, for trusting me and Chekika and Xandor, and for your friendship. I hope you'll always remember to care for this Park which has given you such a beautiful, free, and peaceful place to relax in and camp."

This time they didn't hurry to the boat.

Good, I thought, as we cruised steadily south toward the boat launch. Maybe I've made two new converts to protect our planet. That's what my guiding is all about.

Fellow guide, Leslie Surprenant, and Anne stop for lunch with a Women's Wilderness Workshop.

9

Kestrel Crest Farm

Lila hovered intently above the two electric lines and a power pole that stuck out of the farm pond. Her blue-gray wings quivered rapidly as she shrilled, "*kee, kee, kee.*" The little falcon frolicked in beautiful curves around the object of her attention, swept down to the water's surface, then swooped up to settle atop the tall pole.

A few feet away perched a male. He was smaller, less exuberant, yet sleek and glamorous with his russet back and tail, creamy speckled breast, and lightly tinted, salmon-rose sides. Lila was the more robust and chunky of the two—eleven inches long compared to his nine. And she was definitely the initiator in their April courtship. Suddenly she sprang into the air and flew rapidly to the top of a large tree which marked the southern edge of my farm. She sat swinging on a slender high twig. Now the male shrilled and playfully dove at her. Then he grabbed hold of a twig, too. The two birds rested.

With my binoculars I could plainly see the striking black "moustaches" on the birds' white faces. Their black eyes were ringed in yellow and their heads were crowned with chestnut. To my way of thinking, kestrels are the handsomest of all our falcons. They are the smallest and the most common, too. No other birds of prey can match their maneuvers, save for a cousin, the larger peregrine falcon, with its black helmet and "sideburns" and its sky-scorching flight.

Lila hopped provocatively behind a branch heavy with buds. The male followed. I had no doubt they were mating in their airy bower. Minutes later, Lila flew powerfully toward the utility pole in the pond. She made one sweeping circle as a precaution, then glided precisely into the wood duck nest box nailed there. It was her time to inspect this most peculiar nesting site.

I lowered my binocs and sighed contentedly. It was the fourth spring since I'd purchased my alternate winter residence that the kestrels had nested here. To me, they meant the start of spring and a ritual as passionate and elegant as any in the bird world. Days, I'd watch them hovering on streamlined pointed wings above the surrounding hay fields. *"Killy, killy, killy,"* they shrieked; or else squeaked like mice. Then came the abrupt power dive, the pounce, and the capture of a grasshopper or vole. Nights, if the heat indoors drove me and the dogs to the gazebo to sleep, I often startled the male, who slept under its roof. He'd glare at me reproachfully with luminous dark eyes before jetting off into the night. From the gazebo he could keep watch on his beloved close by in her nest box. I called the male, "Windhover," an old-time colloquial name and the title of a 19th-century poem by Gerard Manley Hopkins.

When I bought the farm, I purposely waited a year before naming it. I wanted to see which wild creature, plant, or natural event most evoked the essence of this place. The kestrels won, wings down. So I called it "Kestrel Crest Farm."

I'd found the ramshackle homestead after searching for three summers around the Lake Champlain valley. A great deal of thought went into this hunt. My lecturing, consulting, and book business were growing and expanding nationally and internationally. It was harder and harder to manage parts of them from my remote cabin in winter.

Kestrel Crest Farm

Ask yourself, dear reader, how you would manage on a January day with wind chill of −22°F, trying to prepare for a lecture trip, say, to West Virginia University? You'd have to sort your slides using a flashlight, pack a suitcase with neat business clothes, prepare at least two boxes of books for autograph parties, plus a slide projector, carousel trays, a handbag with tickets and money, food for the dogs whether they stayed at a kennel or went with you, two pillows, gifts for possible hostess or friend, and a decent winter coat and boots. All this would be heaped onto a toboggan to be pulled over the ice, two miles down the lake, all the while hoping a blizzard or rainstorm wouldn't turn the trip treacherous. Always there lurked the questions: Would the truck start? Was the road plowed? Could you drive up the hilly, winding road if it was icy? Finally, there'd be a plane or train to catch hours away, with the professional obligation to arrive on time and in good shape.

Thus, logistically, I needed a place to work that was near a road, with electricity (to run projector, iron fancy clothes), a phone and fax (for winter book orders), and proximity by turnpike to an airport (two hours drive max). It was important to review my slides on a large screen with a projector. Also, I needed more space to store boxes of my books, writing and business files, and outdoor gear. My guiding service maintained four or five sleeping bags, pads, tents, life vests, and a lot of cooking gear.

On another, more elemental and ecological level, I craved winters with more sun, less acid rain and snow, and milder temps, and summers with a longer growing season. A country place with good soil and spring water would enable me to grow much of my food and pump my own water—without pesticides, chemicals, or chlorine. Self-sufficiency was uppermost in my mind, as was good health.

The final professional requirement was that I stay

inside the Adirondack Park, and within an hour's drive of the Adirondack Park Agency headquarters. Lately I'd taken on more responsibility as a commissioner (one of eleven) of this state agency. I chaired both Regulatory Affairs and Park Ecology committees. Therefore, I had to be at the APA office for meetings every two weeks, or roughly four days out of every month. My work was intensely interesting, and I loved land-use planning.

Imagine, again, my reader, how it could drain your energy and effectiveness to head out from the cabin by boat or snowshoe over Black Bear Lake at 6:00 A.M. Drive two to three hours over mountain roads across the Park, and arrive well-dressed, hair curled, with one to two feet of papers and transcripts under your arm—all carefully read and marked up—for these public meetings. Anyone, from reporters to television crews to guests to a class of students, might be there. Not to mention our staff, a flock of lawyers, and applicants seeking permits or legal advice.

As long as I remained a commissioner and was deeply involved in the environmental protection of this six-million-acre park, as mandated by our governor, I needed to live in it full-time.

I focused my search on the eastern Adirondacks in the rain-and-snow shadow of the High Peaks. There'd be much less precipitation here than in the western Adirondacks. Furthermore, some land lay below 500 feet elevation, which meant a longer frost-free season. The area I chose had both these ecological characteristics, as well as a very pretty landscape. The only aspect I neglected to look into was the sociological flavor of the place.

Now, lest the reader think that I'd sold my cabin and was moving permanently into a more civilized setting, let me hasten to say, NO! The cabin is still my primary permanent residence. It is my writing studio and retreat, my spiritual sanctuary, my sacred space—

much as his cabin in Kentucky was for Thomas Merton, the priest, hermit, and author. I have no intention of ever leaving and built it to last my lifetime.

Nevertheless on April 18, 1988, I drove along a dirt road and up the narrow drive to the crest where my "new" old farmhouse stood. The large stretch of lawn and nearby hay fields were already greening up, although, patches of snow lingered in the ditches and gullies. I noted two kestrels flying above a big tree. They had just arrived to build a temporary home for summer, whereas I had just arrived to prepare a temporary home for winter.

From the crest, I could look out toward the Green Mountains of Vermont. Lake Champlain lay hidden in the deep fold between New York and this adjacent state. The mountains stretched away in shades of denim blue and mauve. I eased out of the truck and walked with the dogs to the farm pond. It looked powder blue under the early spring sky. A fringe of cattails poked like platinum spikes from the cold water. The sun was setting behind me while red-wings whistled cheerily.

I'd driven a long way, having taken all my mother's furniture—she was now deceased—out of storage and directed it to be loaded onto a Mayflower moving van. This van was en route from Miami and due in two days. The driver had made me sign a tough contract, stating that if no one was home to accept the shipment and open the house on April 20, my load would be taken to the nearest city and put into storage. I'd be charged a $1,000 fee to get it released and redelivered.

I had one day to clean the house, make a floor plan for rugs and furniture, and arrange for electricity, phone, and water. Unlocking the door, I moved swiftly through the two-story, empty, cold, dank, smelly building. I suddenly realized I might have made one of the worst mistakes of my life!

The place was filthy! No welcome note from the

past owner awaited me. No instructions lay on the counter about anything. I'd purchased the 85-year-old farmhouse after only two visits and barely knew where the water pump, master fuse box, garage keys, or septic system were. Foolishly I'd relied on the charitable instincts of the owner to help me get situated. However, we had conducted the sale via long-distance through lawyers. I was tired of searching. The price was quite reasonable. It was high time to stop storing my mother's possessions. Maybe the owner was still smarting from the low price he got and decided, "Let her find out for herself."

Find out I did that afternoon and evening. Huge water marks stained every ceiling inside. The roof showed shabby shingles with probably dozens of leaks. Cobwebs and dust piles were everywhere. Scarred, old, gray linoleum covered the floors. Yet when I'd visited earlier, carpeting and antique pieces had given an ambiance of a "quaint old farmstead."

The upstairs bathroom was indescribable. Its washbowl was lined with grime and moustache clippings. The tub was ringed with dirt and black pubic hairs. The hot water line didn't work. A bare bulb overhead was burned out. A pair of disgusting jockey shorts was shoved under a pipe that leaked. In the kitchen, several burned-out pots stood atop the electric stove. Its oven was crusted with blackened remains. The living room seemed narrow and dark, with wind rattling loose windows. The only sign of instructions was an old note taped to the dial of a kerosene heater. It read: "Run on HIGH or stove will smoke up room."

I pictured my mother's Miami-white sofas and flowered easy chairs turning sooty while I tried to warm the living room. Slumping down on the cold linoleum, I tried not to bawl. The thermometer read 40°F, and I wondered where I'd sleep. Stiffly getting up, I ran out to the truck and brought in my sleeping bag, pillows and pad. Then I planned an assault on the house, making a long list of "Things To Do."

Before it got dark, I went back outside and looked around the out-buildings. They were equally trashed-out. More old clothes, used as car rags and a dog's bed, were strewn about the porch. A kerosene tank leaned drunkenly to one side in its cradle. The gauge read *Empty*. Bullet holes and shell casings were everywhere. What in the world did the previous inhabitants shoot at? An abandoned tractor with two flat tires sat in the garage. Paint cans, old glass jars filled with nails and screws, work-worn hand tools, and stacks of newspapers were jammed there, too. To my horror, I found the garden shed held chemical pesticides and fertilizers of every dangerous description—malathion, Eldrin, Sevin, DDT, and much more. I shuddered and shut the door. Why hadn't I noticed any of this? Why hadn't the owner cleaned the place up before moving out? Wasn't it an obligation, a courtesy, a nicety, to give the new owner a clean home to come into? No answers came to me.

I went back inside, ate a sandwich (afraid to turn on the stove), fed the dogs, and placed my sleeping gear in the least dirty room. My last thought before going to sleep was, "It'll all look better when my own things are in place."

April 19 found me scurrying from room to room in rubber gloves, with a bandana over my nose and mouth, carrying pails of soapy water mixed with Comet, Clorox, and Mr. Clean, plus dusters and brooms. The dogs were tied outdoors, for fear they'd irritate their paws on the scrubbed floors. By afternoon, the smell of cleansers was positively toxic. But the bathroom glistened. Every room was free of cobwebs and dust balls. Windows shone. The power was on. So was the water pump.

Around 5:00 P.M., the real estate agent stopped by on her way home from work. After one quick whiff, she exclaimed, "Anne, you *have* to get out of here! It's unhealthy! Come home with me. Let's have a scotch, a steak, and a good sleep. The house should air out. You can come back early and be ready for that van."

Bless her heart. I did just that. Right after I returned the next day, the Mayflower truck edged up the narrow drive. The driver was yelling at his assistant for not directing him properly. He'd already sideswiped one forsythia bush. The men seemed in a terrible hurry to unload. They rushed in and out with boxes, chairs, throw rugs, and dressers, snapping at me to show them where to place these items.

When they tried to carry my mother's (and grandmother's and great aunt Annie's) mahogany bed upstairs, we reached our first impasse. The headboard wouldn't fit up the narrow stairwell. The two men sweated and glared.

"Where do you want it?" one asked.

"In the bedroom, upper right," I moaned. "Let me get my chain saw and I'll cut it in half. I can nail and glue it back together later." (I was still in my cabin mentality).

"Naw," the driver said. "That's stupid. Nice bed. Old bed. I'll store it in the garage for now."

When they tried to manhandle my mother's heavy oak desk into the office-to-be, it wouldn't pass through the door. This time I did get my saw and take two inches off each of the eight legs. Now the desk fit and it didn't wobble.

The living room rugs were wet from a transient storm that had leaked into the van, but we had to lay them down anyway. I'd never have managed alone. Somehow we finished by 5:00 P.M. The driver urged me to sign this paper, then that one, so he could depart. "Got to get to the next city," he said. "I'm paying this guy overtime now. You satisfied, lady?"

He looked at me expectantly. It had been a *dreadful* experience for me. Such impersonality and impatience. But then I'd never moved a household before. Maybe this was the way movers acted as they rushed people's belongings all over America in this lonely, peripatetic society. His posture suggested he was waiting for a tip. I gave him fifty dollars. "Share it with your helper," I reminded him.

The driver mumbled thanks and raced outside. Both men got in the truck, he backed it onto the rain-soft lawn—and began to sink in. An hour later, having made ruts almost a foot deep, he relented and called a tow truck. That fifty dollars disappeared fast. The driver gave me more papers to sign in case I wanted to put in a claim to the company for damages. I did.

After their motor noise died away the silence was palpable. The old house smelled clean. Spring sunshine slanted through tall old windows. My family mementos and furniture—so long in storage—felt friendly around me. They completely filled the six small rooms. I needed to buy nothing! The dogs dozed on the damp pastel rugs. I tried to imagine what the cabin looked like right now. It would certainly be freezing cold with some snow and ice on the ground and lake. No birds would be singing. Not a sign of green anywhere. However, my sleeping loft would look enticing with its down quilt and woolen blankets. I started to feel homesick. No! That would never do. Grabbing my sleeping gear, I fixed a spot on the floor upstairs where the old bed was supposed to go. And that's where I would sleep off and on for the next nine months.

Little by little over the next three years, as my finances allowed, I fixed up the farmhouse: New metal roof, a wood stove, white paint for the ceilings, bright curtains, flowered wallpaper, a wrap-around sun deck, one picture window, modern vinyl in the kitchen, and much more. The real coup was finding a carpenter willing to cut through the upstairs wall, haul my mother's bed up and in with ropes, and then install two small windows. Finally I had a familiar bed to sleep in, and the hallway and stairwell were flooded with sun in the afternoons. The second floor became a cheery haven. I also made a dent in the cluttered outbuildings. There were two huge, 85-year-old barns with connecting workroom, a tottering chicken coop, the pesticide-filled garden shed, and the garbage-clogged garage. Each was filled with stacks of magazines, old lumber, broken furniture, vehicles, and cracked dishes, apparently having served as residential dump sites for each of the owners. I must have taken hundreds of loads of junk to the local landfill. I also sold 7,000 pounds of old metal to a scrap dealer, disposed of the chemicals responsibly, and burned piles of trash.

I never stopped working. Many good friends came to see my new place—and helped clean. I never got bored on that farm. Winters I had projects galore. What had I done with all those idle winter hours at the cabin, I wondered, besides carry firewood and shovel snow and write? Life there seemed so simple, restful, and unpretentious. Nothing like log walls, three Navajo rugs, and furniture made with a chain saw to cut down on household demands.

Every once in a while, when I snooped through my big barns, an overwhelming urge to keep animals here swept over me. I pictured throwing grain to free-roaming hens from a renovated chicken coop and collecting their rich organic eggs. Piglets, I learned, were adorable and smart as shepherds. If I raised a couple, maybe they'd play with my dogs. My saddles and bridles from my hotel days were stored at my cabin. There was enough grass around the barns to feed a horse. Maybe I should buy one and begin riding again. Then the certain knowledge that owning animals meant getting tied down to a daily and yearly feeding routine swept this silliness from my mind. It was all pie in the sky, nourished by the bucolic, rural setting where I now lived part-time. I couldn't continue to live at my cabin *and* raise animals. I was a woodswoman at heart, a wilderness guide, a wildlife ecologist—and I always would be.

Kestrel Crest Farm

Other new and satisfying compensations, however, filled those early spring days. Dawns blushing soft, pink, misty, fresh, and alive with hundreds of bird songs. Bluebirds nesting in a box right out the kitchen window. Tree swallows by the dozen liquidly twittering to their young lined up on the electric wires. Bass surfacing in the pond under willows while peepers trilled. Red-and-brown house finches frivolously rearing a total of 12 chicks on my front porch. Sober gray phoebes dutifully feeding four fuzzballs in a nest over the night light on my back porch. Wood frogs clacking and woodcocks peeting on cold, clear spring evenings under a half moon.

Every spring thereafter Lila and Windhover would show up to perform their glorious courtship. They trusted my farm and its wood duck box, strangely-placed on a power pole in a pond, as their rightful nursery and home. It seemed providential when the U.S. Postal Service printed one-cent stamps with an American Kestrel on them. Now I could seal my envelopes with a Kestrel stamp and write "Kestrel Crest Farm" under it—my own special "emblem." More and more I began to identify with these small, strong, defiant falcons, flying into the wind.

10

The Farm and the Cabin

Working on an old farmstead part-time taught me new and insightful lessons about Nature. It threw certain "ecological imperatives" into my lap. And it showed me the dramatic contrast between cabin and farm. I gradually came to realize that my 30 acres of old-growth forest bordered in back by wilderness and fronted by a remote, roadless lake doesn't need me for anything. The natural resources are stable, diverse, and have been in place since the last Ice Age. The biological laws function well here. I take very little from the land and the land takes very little from me. I don't try to change or domesticate my surroundings. I never feel "in charge" of these wildlands, since they "belong" to a larger complex ecosystem and not to a mere human landowner.

Now and then I cut a few trees (preferably deformed or dead) for firewood, posts, or a roof support. Each fall I renew the posted signs for my wildlife refuge to protect animals from trespassers, hunters, and trappers. That's about it. I'm much more a spectator of nature here, watching loons and beavers, listening to owls and coyotes. This makes me feel a greater part of the natural ecosystem than I am at my farm.

On the farm, however, I am constantly manipulating this cut-over, farmed, pastured, open land. And the land is manipulating me. I have planted 1,800 tree seedlings in the course of eight years, trying to make windbreaks, stabilize banks and ditches, provide privacy, and turn worn-out fields into wildlife habitat. The Scotch pines, European larch, poplars and many bushes that provide food for wildlife are exotics from other areas or countries. On one hand, I feel this has upset the original environment. On the other, I know that both exotic and native species of trees make soil more stable, useful, and attractive. They also counteract effects of global warming.

Still, the overall effect is to make me feel that I'm domesticating nature and putting my imprint on it. True, this work gives me pleasure, new vistas, vegetables and fruit, honey and bass, nesting birds. Yet somehow this work distances me from that pure, exhilarating sensation of being part of a primeval community in the wilderness. That mystical sense of communion with raw Life.

At Black Bear Lake I never poison the waters to remove trash fish, treat aquatic weeds, or stock new fish. All I do is dip in buckets for drinking water. Yet at my farm pond, I use Aquashade to discourage pond weeds, I cut back cattails, and I stock bass to improve my little bass fishery. It's definitely domestication.

At West of the Wind, there are no lawns, gardens, fruit trees, berry bushes, or bee hives. I hug big white pines and listen to the wind in the conifers; pick fall leaves or wild spring azaleas along the roadsides; glean raspberries from forest clearings. At Kestrel Crest Farm, my life is dictated by the great Imperatives of Green Grass, Weeds, and Fruit. These are demanding, daunting labor laws.

The farmhouse and pond are surrounded by five acres of rolling, lush lawn. It was here when I came and it's so lovely that it's going to stay. I'm well aware of current ecological criticism against Americans' mania for green grass, against the use of chemical herbicides, fertilizers, and lawn services that contaminate ground water and poison birds. I know about the millions of gallons of gas and oil burned to run mowers and weed whackers each summer in the United States and the air pollution and acid rain they cause. None of these machines have catalytic converters, filters, or any other device to cleanse nitrous oxides from their exhausts. Carelessly operated mowers and weed whackers also kill thousands of ground-nesting birds, chicks, frogs, small snakes, and rodents with their whirring blades. So I do all I can to reduce the effects of mowing by cutting back the size of my lawns, keeping the new 18 HP riding tractor with its 48-inch deck well serviced and changing oil frequently. I study how to mow in strategic, time-saving patterns to save gas, and keep a sharp eye out for ground-hugging critters. Often I go out of my way to avoid them. I mow only when really necessary, about ten times per season. Luckily, I've found careful handymen to do the job when I am tied down at the cabin. Still, it is one of the most demanding tasks at my farm.

On the positive side, mowing becomes the most wonderful way to know my land. Seated three feet above the ground, moving at a sensibly slow speed, the sky stretching limitless over my head, and the sun bronzing my skin—I consider it a majestic experience. Alabaster thunderheads sail by. Rainbows come and go. White seagulls dot the distant hayfields. The wind sweeps up from Lake Champlain—cool, damp, and smelling faintly of clay.

Sometimes I pinpoint a pesky rock, waiting to blunt the blades. I hop off and spray-paint it red. Other times I find gypsy moth cocoons in the mulberry bushes or apple trees. Again, I hop off to break the branches and stomp the caterpillars under my boots. A raven feather may lie glistening on the pond's sand beach. I pick it up and attach it to one pigtail, Indian-style. The average person would never take time with such trivia. But my tractor, which I named *La Tortuga* (turtle in Spanish), allows me to keep my fingertips on the pulse of the land.

The Farm and the Cabin

On July evenings when the dew is light and the breeze is strong, I sometimes turn on its headlights and mow into the dusky twilight and eventual dark. That's when the lawn turns into a sparkling carpet of fireflies. Since these insects only live three weeks or so, the sight is a breath-taking treat—one I never see at the cabin. Male fireflies fly up, beaming an upward J-stroke of light every five or six seconds. The females huddle in the grass to watch, hanging onto blades with their six tiny feet. If one likes what she sees, she'll flash back—exactly 2.7 seconds after the male sparks off. If he feels interested, he'll flash again every 5.7 seconds, drawing nearer. The female may then maintain a steady series of bright flashes every 2.7 seconds. This precise Morse code of mating is what turns them on.

How many kids know about this secret sex life of fireflies? I never did as a child, lying in bed with my jar of glowing bugs on the night table. I'm too mature now to collect them; however, the sight of courting fireflies in the lawn still seems a fantasy. At such times, Mr. Xandor plods behind me doggedly wondering when he'll get his supper. It's ten o'clock and his mistress is still going 'round in circles on that infernal noisy machine—mesmerized.

Another Imperative is Weeds in the Gardens. What a surprise it was to discover that I love green plants and gardening. Maybe it's a displaced "raising animals" syndrome. Domestic plants are not that different from domestic animals. They both need to be watered, kept in a clean space, and treated well (until you eat them). Yet plants take less care since they don't move around much (though some of my acorn squash have meandered fifteen feet over a summer). They function in a completely different time frame and with a different type of nervous system. I wish to tune in on it, but can't quite—yet.

A revelation swept through my mind, heart, and stomach the first time I watched bare soil sprouting with the fragile green leaves of lettuce, Swiss chard, carrots, beets, dill, beans, radishes, corn, and spinach. The knowledge that I'd be eating fully grown garden produce in a few weeks—food that looked like the colored pictures on the front of seed packets—was awesome. The realization that I had poked tiny seeds into warm, moist earth, covered them, and let sun and rain nourish them into ripe, edible plant food ready to be picked was inspiring. It struck me how closely the reproduction of higher plants resembles the reproduction of mammals. All begin as mere specks of living matter. A puppy or baby begins roughly the same way as a plant, when sperm are introduced to eggs in a womb's warm, moist environment, then nourished by the mother until they are born. And so, like Thoreau, "I came to love my rows, my beans...They attached me to the earth, and so I got strength like Antaeus."

I learned to fight weeds so as to have better plant progeny. Sometimes I'd weed through the hot, hazy afternoon until the long-shafted rays of the sun gilded every leaf. I'd glance up at the phoebes calling in the mulberry bushes and the cedar waxwings lisping in the dead elms. Sometimes I'd stay out in the vegetable or flower gardens until it was so dark that the end of the hoe or cultivator disappeared. Only then would I stop so as not to spear my bare toes.

"This was my curious labor all summer,..." wrote Thoreau, "to make this portion of the earth's surface, which had yielded only...sweet wild fruits and pleasant flowers, produce instead this pulse." "...making the earth say beans instead of grass,..." (In my case it was blue corn instead of beans.)

Often I ached with painful longing for a lost love in another country. This happened especially in the long, long twilights of June. The weeds were there to focus my immediate attention while my thoughts drifted all over the world. Up and down the rows I'd grub—past blue corn with a small fish buried beneath each stalk,

In June my vegetable garden was covered with rows of roofing to keep out weeds. The first tiny seedlings are peeking up in between.

alongside zinnias as colorful as a carnival, next to lettuce leaves as translucent as pale green emeralds. This twilight nostalgia was a combination of loneliness, *welt-schmertz,* and country contentment.

I manage to wipe out most of the weeds to help my plants. Contrarily, the local wildlife destroys some of my food and flower supply. Baby brown bunnies sneak through the fencing to nibble crisp sweet lettuce. Coons scramble over the fence top and up corn stalks to rip off the juicy cobs. Tiny mice leave toothmarks

By September my blue corn was "high as an elephant's eye!"

ringing the tops of beets. Jays peck off sunflower seeds before I can salvage any. Colorado potato bugs munch away leaves on every potato plant. Chipmunks steal crocus bulbs and half the tulips. Deer would have gobbled everything in sight except that Chekika and Xandor have turned out to be the best garden protectors. Xandor methodically marks the fences and Chekika frequently barks boisterously.

Henry David Thoreau was a lucky gardener. He reported, "My enemies are worms, cool days, and most of all woodchucks."

All this hard work is painful. I always have an aching muscle, cut, or bruise bothering me on this farm. I have quickly learned how difficult a farmer's life can be. After that first long summer my opinion of farmers rose to one of highest respect. No other work, save maybe ranching and commercial fishing, demands such dedication and drive. It is also dangerous. A nearby neighbor tipped his farm tractor over in the woods and pinned his right thigh beneath the motor block. He dug himself out with bare hands and nails, then spent weeks hobbling about with a badly swollen leg.

During the short periods I work at the farm in summer, I have witnessed great fluctuations and unexpected violence from the weather. One year frequent thunderstorms with terrifying black squall lines and scary lightning moved across the Champlain Valley. (No wonder my house and barns had lightning rods all along the ridgepoles and atop the chimneys.) Another summer, the drought was so severe that I had to haul dozens of buckets of water from my pond to the gardens and little trees to save them. The pond level dropped five feet, so that eventually I walked right across the bottom with my head above the surface where it is normally ten feet deep. Some months the wind blew so hard that the old house shuddered and thrummed as if about to collapse. Another year, the precipitation was so high that my basement filled with

The Farm and the Cabin 133

18 inches of water and small ditches roared like rivers. Even the Lake Champlain ferry landings were flooded, and transportation stopped. Nature holds out no guarantees to farmers or landowners around here. The agricultural land and woodlots lack the ancientness, timelessness, and built-in safeguards of old-growth forests.

I've never felt the unpredictability of Nature as keenly as I do at the farm. I keep hoping for a "normal" year, but there never is one. Winters are just as unpredictable as summers. Once, the temperatures were so low and the mouse population so high that 40 percent of the small pines I'd planted were girdled and died. Another winter brought freezing rain and crusted snow week after week. From my living room, I watched two starving coyotes with bushy tails wander over the stone-hard snow, repeatedly pouncing stiff-legged onto the surface, trying to break through. Inches below their paws was a world of rodents that could have fed them until spring. While wildlife cycles are common among many species and weather fluctuations are always expected, here in the Champlain Valley they seem accentuated. The balance of Nature is continually thrown off.

Here, too, I've seen some of the saddest sights I'd ever known. I opened my wood stove in July one day, thinking I heard something rustling inside. Thirteen starlings—twelve dead and one about to die—lay in grotesque attitudes among the ashes. They'd died of thirst and starvation in that squat iron prison whose only exit was a shiny metal pipe running straight up for 30 feet. No young bird could have flown out. But these fledglings somehow flew or fell in, perhaps from a nest built inside the stove cap. I pictured their panic, the slow energy loss, the beating of wings. Do birds ever pray to a Higher Being? Did they cry for their mother? I picked each one out, putting them in a paper bag. It weighed next to nothing. That fall, I phoned my chimney sweep and had him install a new stove cap with wire mesh sides onto the stove pipe to prevent any birds, exotic or native, from falling down it. It cost almost fifty dollars, but it was worth it. It was my guilt price.

One afternoon, mowing about the barns, I saw a dead bird near the road by the old milkhouse door. I stopped to pick it up and found one of Lila's and Windhover's fledglings. The feathers were perfectly placed, no blood, the colors and moustaches so pretty. Grief-stricken, I looked around for what might have killed it. The only explanation, finally, was that the youngster had been hovering too near the barns, a car drove by, and the frightened falcon dashed itself into the wall.

The dutiful nesting phoebes also met disaster. One dawn I heard the female calling over and over from a locust tree near the back porch. So insistent was her noise that I climbed cautiously onto a chair to feel inside her nest over the porch light. Nothing there! Mystified, I consulted with my neighbor, Dean, who knows all there is to know about ornithology. He couldn't figure it out, since no cat could climb the aluminum-sided walls and my back porch seemed too sheltered for a bird of prey to enter.

The poor pair kept up their plaintive crying all that day. Next morning they were still staying close to the nest over the night light. I began to smell a rotten odor nearby. Looking inside a giant old earthenware crock that I keep by the back door for umbrellas, cross-country skiis, and walking sticks, I discovered two fuzzy dead chicks with lacerations on their backs and wings. I retrieved them and started searching over the lawn. Between the garage and pond, I found another, similarly wounded, chick. Finally, at noon, when I went to take a dip with the dogs, the fourth met my eyes. It was floating head down in the pond.

Dean and I pieced the puzzle together. A Cooper's hawk had been harassing his bird feeders, picking off a sparrow or finch now and then. Undoubtedly the hawk noticed the frequent feeding pattern of the phoebe parents and pinpointed the nest. At first light, the hawk had braved my narrow back porch to circle in, grab the four chicks in its beak, and try to fly away—only it pecked off more than it could swallow. It had to drop the struggling babies as it flew into the forest, leaving a trail of carnage and waste. That hawk didn't win a meal; the phoebes lost their family. They stayed in mourning the rest of that summer.

My hypothesis for the violent weather, the fluctuations in fecundity, and the wildlife cycles I've experienced in the Champlain Valley has to do in part with the monocultures making up this landscape. Such farming practices are atypical of the rest of the Adirondack Park. Here, fields are devoted solely to corn, or hay, or birdsfoot trefoil. Farms are stocked only with cows, or sheep, or horses. Woodlots are composed mostly of white or Scotch pines, or maple trees. When a rich diversity of plants and animals is lacking, a natural disaster can wipe out a single crop or farm animal far more easily than if many plants and animals exist in a tight-knit association. Just as with a widely diversified portfolio, some investments are always sound; with high biodiversity, some species always survive.

The other part of my hypothesis hints at a grimmer reason for the volatile weather. As our climate warms from air pollution, as the ozone hole expands, and as CFCs (chlorofluorocarbons, or refrigerant gases), continue to nibble away at the ozone layer, the earth will experience more violent changes. Weather fronts will roar through with higher winds, more precipitation, and more significant ups and downs in barometer and temperature readings, than we experience now. It's inevitable.

Meanwhile, I do enjoy a few precious summer evenings relaxing on the sun porch. I revel in the plush velvet perfection of newly cut lawn atwinkle with fireflies. I sniff the large bouquets of old-fashioned farm flowers which I pick and place on the dining room table—sweet-smelling phlox, day lilies, blue delphiniums, bee balm, and yellow tea roses. Best of all is when I can eat a light supper from my garden: dill and lettuce salad, fresh corn on the cob, new potatoes, and ripe raspberries. In these shining contented moments, life is good.

Come autumn, the Imperative of Ripe Fruits arrives. Every time I drive to the farm in September or October, some crop *has* to be picked before it gets ruined. I dig potatoes, store carrots and beets in dry sand, hang pails of apples and pears in the basement, fill jars with honey, make jam and jelly, pile squashes in screened drawers, stew applesauce, and bake berry pies. Until now, I had never harvested my own food. What a deeply satisfying experience it is.

Finally, in early November, comes a respite. The farm produce is in, woodpiles are stacked and covered, gladiola bulbs have been dug up, and storm windows have been put on. Small birds come back to my winter feeders. Even haughty ravens stalk pigeon-toed across the frosty lawns, pecking at stale bread chunks. Cluster flies are everywhere indoors. They emerge from the ground about August 28 and begin a steady, sly entry into the house through tiny cracks in walls and windows. They busily buzz and swarm against the windows by day, speckling the glass with dots. At night they huddle in cozy clusters in corners. Come May, they vanish outdoors, leaving me to wash all the glass, inside and out, storm windows too, upstairs and down—an eight-hour task.

Sitting by the woodstove on long winter nights, I rest. And I often think about Rodney. My beloved friend, a master Adirondack guide, died in June 1989, the year after I bought the farm. An extensive operation on his arthritic knees caused him to have a deep brainstem stroke. Over seven long weeks he withered away in the Saranac Lake's Adirondack Medical Center.

Before his operation I'd told Rodney he could come recuperate at the farm, where it was sunny, open, and easy to get around. I even dared to hope that he would start spending winters with me. Kestrel Crest Farm would be a pleasant place for both of us. At 84 years, my "Iron Butterfly" could use a little pampering and companionship. But that dream was not to be. Instead I have his old wood-and-gas stove, the one that we sat by so often in his camp. I salvaged it from his kitchen, carted it down to the farm, installed it in my kitchen, and heaved out that damn electric range. I also brought Rod's down jacket, worn hoe and cultivator, and some of his red seed potatoes. I use these tools in my gardens and his potato line has kept going.

Whenever weather is too raw to be outside or I feel blue, I have only to put on my worn padded Carharts and stout mittens and head into one of my barns. The Augean mess there will take years to clean up.

As restful as winters may be on the farm, they have been much more productive than the ones spent at the cabin. I've written and self-published two books—*The Wilderness World of Anne LaBastille* and *Birds of the Mayas*. Occasionally I give lectures at colleges around the northeast or do book signings at Borders, Barnes & Noble, and smaller book shops. Once each winter I make a trip to Guatemala to renew my research at Lake Atitlán and see old friends. Even though the giant grebes are extinct, many ecological changes are occurring on this gorgeous lake. I need to record these changes and seek a way to restore the original ecosystem, do conservation education, and help the native Maya inhabitants restore their natural resources. And, of course, my bi-weekly meetings at the Adirondack Park Agency go on and on, rain, snow, or shine, as I work to protect the Park from over-development.

Did I say farm winters were restful? Well, sort of...

11

Napoleon's Gift

The Christmas gift arrived early. It was wrapped in exquisite patterns of beige, light blue, cinnamon, forest green, and russet, set off by a band of snow white and decorations of carmine red. The present was a pheasant—a noisy, curious, impudent, arrogant, stealthy, gorgeous pheasant.

I was back at my old farmhouse again, and early winter was a convenient time to perform small, end-of-the-year tasks. I was writing Christmas cards, composing my annual Christmas letter, photocopying, stuffing, stamping, and licking, assembling checks and receipts, preparing IRS materials for my accountant, closing out many bookstore invoices, faxing shopkeepers who still owed money, and finalizing my annual business diary. In short, I was doing all those boring, odious jobs that would have been difficult, if not impossible, to accomplish at my cabin.

The sudden presence of the pheasant was a cheerful diversion. Undoubtedly he had escaped from the flock of hatchery-reared ringnecks released by New York State's Department of Environmental Conservation for the short fall hunting season. These game birds, unused to hay fields and brushland, could scarcely hope to survive. Within days of leaving their pens, most had been either scented by bird dogs and shot by hunters or killed by natural predators or vehicles. Obviously they had never experienced these

Napoleon's Gift

terrors before.

Yet somehow this wily bird had slipped away into the hedge rows, creek beds, ditches and small woodlots of this Champlain Valley farm country. Now here he was, shortly before Christmas, begging for dinner at my back door. If that refugee needed a "safe house" and wanted to dine well, he couldn't have chosen a better locale.

My neighbor Dean and I are both avid bird watchers, photographers, and conservationists. The last thing we'd do is shoot a bird. Rather, we spend hundreds of dollars each winter feeding the rascals. We soon named the pheasant "Napoleon," for his many-colored "uniform," his militaristic little strut, and his strategic maneuvering between our homes.

Napoleon scouted out devious routes from Dean's patio, hung with several overflowing feeders to my side porch strewn with sunflower seeds, stale bread, pie crusts, and breakfast cereal. Daily, he would sneak through a copse of little trees, cross a tiny brook, edge along my hay field, scoot under a windbreak of pines, and then march blatantly down my driveway. Each time Napoleon announced his technicolor presence with a vibrant crowing. Then, the hungry bird would hunker over cracked corn, banana bread, and frosted flakes.

Since Dean had a ferocious goshawk frequenting his feeders, he wanted to protect Napoleon. Pheasant is a favorite food of this raptor. He collected cast-off Christmas trees and formed a camouflaged, curved passageway from the edge of his house to the little woods. Napoleon used it constantly, for we could trace his wobbling, three-toed tracks in the snow.

For my part, I provided protection in the form of Chekika and Xandor, those ferocious shepherds, who patrolled my front lawn for chipmunks, red squirrels, and ravens. They didn't give a damn about finches, blue jays, or pheasants.

One calm cold morning in January, I was sitting on my sun porch writing when I saw Napoleon inching his way across the snow cover with a beautiful buffy female. The dogs watched nonchalantly while both birds began pecking at seeds. Were they a pair? Or had they just met, I wondered. How amazing it would be if this couple had made it through hunting season together. I only glimpsed the hen a few times that month as she was far more skittish than Napoleon.

Then, in February, a neighbor two miles away told me that a lone female was coming to her feeder. Could it be another hen? Or had Napoleon been a shade too overbearing towards his lady?

Winter waned into spring. March in the Champlain Valley brings one day at 60°F with bright sun and the promise of greenery, then the next five with gray clouds, sleet, and wind reminiscent of the Scottish Highlands. On the warm days, Napoleon began an insistent crowing atop some abandoned hay bales between our houses. He made repeated daring advances at Dean's shiny red jeep when it drove by. He scurried back and forth, back and forth between our feeding stations. His strident *kok-cack, kok-cack* was waking us up at 5:30 A.M. Clearly, our pheasant was brimming with testosterone and advertising for a mate. No hens were around. I called my neighbor to ask about her female. Perhaps we could entice her into a Have-A-Heart trap and bring her over to Napoleon. But her pheasant had disappeared.

In early April the snow was gone, and we had a warm spell. One day I'd been doing heavy garden work and felt famished. I decided to drive into town and buy a turkey sub and ice-cold Coke. Headed home down a hill at fifty miles per hour, I saw a cock pheasant dart out in front of my truck. Slamming on the brakes, I screamed with horror and swerved towards the shoulder. I heard a small thud. My dogs cowered in the camper behind the cab. Swiftly I parked and jumped out.

Was it Napoleon? Who else would be cruising around a mile from my house, pretending to be a roadrunner? His great desire for a female must have taken him into unknown and dangerous territory.

Calming my shepherds, I raced back to the site of impact. Brown covert feathers littered the roadway. A few clung to tall dead grass along the side. Plunging down the embankment, I tracked them toward a patch of woods. I heard a loud whir of wings. Silence. Staring at a low tree, I noted a dark mass in it. A squirrel's nest? A bunch of broken branches? Hurrying toward it, I found Napoleon hanging upside down!

Quietly I crept up, my heart in my throat. He's dead, I thought. No bird could withstand being hit with a four-wheel-drive half-ton Chevy! At that instant, the pheasant fell head-first onto the ground, stood up, and sped through a small cattail swamp. Hot in pursuit, I sloshed into the wetland, filling both boots with icy water. No bird. I listened. No noise. Trudging sadly and slowly out of the swamp, I almost stepped on Napoleon. His beige-brown-cream coverts, bronzy body, and green head blended perfectly with the winter-bleached sedges and cattails. Only the powder-blue feathers over his lower back gave him away in that bleak landscape.

Immediately, I wrenched off my padded flannel shirt and flung it over the immobile bird. Napoleon gave one low, hoarse, alarm grunt. I picked him up gently, wrapped him in the shirt with wings tight to his body, and carried him back to my truck. I laid him on the floor in the cab under the heater, then ordered Chekika and Xandor to stay in the back.

My EMT and first aid training said, treat for shock, keep the patient warm and quiet, reassure, no fluids. So I turned on the heater, clucked soothingly to Napoleon, and shot back to town. A vet wildlife rehabilitator had an office there. But the receptionist stated that she was out until 3:30 P.M. Frantically I tried to decide what to do. Someone needed to evaluate Napoleon's injuries. Did the bird have many broken bones? Was he bleeding? I was too shaken to try to find out. And so my beautiful pheasant friend stayed like an anonymous lump on the truck floor with his head up a shirt sleeve.

I drove home, took two aspirins, ate the sub, drank the Coke, and let Napoleon rest in the truck. Wild birds can die from stress so swiftly: loud noises, temperature changes, blood loss, harsh blows, or excess handling. Napoleon had suffered all of these, plus hanging upside down in a tree and huddling in icy water.

At 3:15 P.M. he was still alive, blinking at me steadily with clear amber eyes from inside the sleeve. The dogs, pheasant, and I drove back to the vet's office. I began to hope that just maybe his injuries were superficial, not catastrophic. As I waited, I cradled Napoleon close to my chest so my warmth would help him. It was like holding a treasure—that flamboyant, fragile, elegant, brilliant bird.

Shortly after 5:00 P.M., the vet summoned me in. By then I had called Dean and told him the disturbing news. "Come over if you can," I pleaded. "I'm so upset! Napoleon's been hit and has been suffering for five hours. It's all my fault." Tears welled up in my eyes.

Dean was there in fifteen minutes, camera and flash in hand. "You didn't mean to hit him," he said comfortingly. "Maybe he'll be okay."

"Sorry you had to wait," said the vet, beckoning us into an examining room. "I have to take paying patients, like dogs and cats, first. Wildlife is seen free of charge since all wild animals belong to the public."

"I'd be glad to pay for an office visit and medicine," I volunteered at once.

"Can't do that," she said matter-of-factly. "The State won't let us. But donations for our rehabilitation work are always welcome."

After a thorough exam, she pronounced Napoleon's short wide wings, long spurred legs, and gorgeous banded neck in working order. But the lower back area and the top of his head had taken the blow. The skin had been ripped off the back; however, the back muscles were not torn and the skull was not fractured, so I hoped his brain was all right. "This handsome fellow should be able to strut and court again," she smiled. "Right now, hypothermia and infection where there's no feathers or skin covering are our major concern. I'll just see if I can piece him together."

Napoleon chose that moment to make a dash for it. He wiggled his wings loose and flapped wildly, but the doctor held on tight to his legs. "Time to get to work," she announced.

Tanks of anaesthetic and oxygen were wheeled in. An assistant scrubbed the top of the examining table clean. Then she placed a plastic hood over the pheasant's head. "I'm giving him a gas called ISO," explained the vet. "Same thing as humans get."

Gradually Napoleon's amber eyes drooped and his blinking slowed. The gaudy head nodded. "It's the only thing I dare use safely to ease the pain," she explained. "An IV might kill him. There's not a whole lot known about anaesthesia and surgery for pheasants."

The small, slender vet began to stitch Napoleon's shredded, tissuey skin back across his body. She worked like an expert quilter, taking first one scrap, then another still attached, and piecing them artfully together. She rearranged, stitched some more, and eyed the pattern. The needle was a tiny sliver of curved steel; the suturing thread like a delicate cobweb. Dean and I were stunned by her precision, daring, and medical expertise. Finally, the pheasant's back was almost covered with protective flesh.

Now she daubed Nolvosan antiseptic ointment liberally over his lower back. Another dollop of the creamy antiseptic was smeared on top of his head.

"This will feel soothing to him," she murmured. She peered closely at the horseshoe-shaped flap of skin atop the skull which was held neatly in place by dried blood. Then she gently stroked the lovely light blue feathers into place across the repaired skin. Nodding in a satisfied way, she reached over and turned off the gas tanks.

Shortly after she removed the hood, Napoleon lifted his eyelids and regarded us suspiciously. I tried to imagine the intense pain he'd endured for the last six hours. And the bird had never grunted, or cried, or... anything. Surely wild creatures must have enormous reserves of stamina and those mysterious, internal pain-deadeners, endorphins.

"How long will he have to stay here?" asked Dean.

The vet picked up Napoleon, wrapped him back up in my old shirt, and stuck him comfortably under her left arm. "Not long. Let's look at what's available in the indoor cages."

We followed her to the boarding section. Several breeds of dogs peered out and whined. "I don't feel comfortable leaving him in any of these dog pens. The pheasant could stick his head through the wire mesh and choke. Also, the barking will frighten him." She glanced out the window at a thermometer, "It's too cold outdoors to put him in a wildlife pen—not after what he's been through." I noted the temperature had dropped to 40°F.

"Let me bring one of my dogs' airline kennels over," I offered. "The wire mesh is smaller."

Napoleon kicked his legs vigorously under the shirt, as if *he* had something to say in the matter of his hospital room.

"This bird is really strong," the vet remarked again. "It's all that spring testosterone. In fact," she paused, "he may be well enough to go home with you."

"I think I can solve the problem," said Dean. "There's an old chicken coop on my property. The

Wildlife rehabilitator, Dr. Sue Russell supports Napoleon after his operation. Her young daughter assisted. *Photo by: Dean Spaulding*

doors and windows are tight. Just some hay and cardboard boxes inside. He'd be out of the cold and rain. We can fix him a nest."

"Can you cover the windows?" asked the vet. "We don't want Napoleon flying into the glass and breaking his neck after all this surgery."

"Sure," replied Dean. "I've got some old blankets and feed sacks around. We can nail them up."

"It's only a five-minute walk from my house to Dean's," I added. "We can take turns feeding and caring for him. And there is *plenty* of bird food."

"Try to bring him in a couple of times over the next ten days," advised the vet, "so I can check his wounds for infection. But if he stresses out too much when you try to catch him," she warned, "just let him be."

So it was settled. I slipped over to the office desk to leave a generous donation. Wearily I picked up Napoleon and laid him carefully on the floor of my truck again. His head had slipped back into the shirt sleeve. Then I eased behind the wheel and followed Dean's jeep to his home.

In the hour before dusk, we transformed the chicken coop into a pheasant convalescent center. We laid one big box upside down and scattered cracked corn and millet seed atop this makeshift table. I filled a dog dish with water while Dean mounded hay into nests on the floor and up on a shelf beside one small window. He left a tiny pane exposed so Napoleon could have a sun bath every afternoon. "It may help him heal faster," he reasoned, "if he can glimpse the real world out there."

Finally, just at dark, I unwrapped the quiet bird and set him down on his nest. Instantly, he flattened himself, tucked his head under the hay, and disappeared. "Nighty-night," I whispered as we closed the door.

As I walked home through the chilly spring night, my heart was overflowing with relief and gratitude. The guilt of having nearly killed Napoleon, our friendly pheasant, was too awful to think about. What good fortune it was to find an experienced wildlife rehabilitator and to have a great neighbor. I opened my back door and let the dogs in, gave them each a big hug and praise for their patience, and fixed them an especially tasty dinner.

The week passed quickly. Every time Dean or I entered the chicken coop Napoleon would be crouching by the uncovered pane of glass, staring into the fields. We would check to see whether he'd eaten his corn, drunk water, and defecated. All appeared normal.

Napoleon's Gift

After the third day, we decided to take him back for a checkup.

I crept up onto the broad shelf where the bird reclined and silently inched towards him with my old quilted shirt. At the second I lunged, Napoleon streaked to the other side of the coop. His speed and agitated stare convinced us he'd not be caught that day...or the next, or the next. Finally I called the vet.

"Forget it!" she exclaimed. "If he's that agile and alert, he doesn't have an infection. I don't want to take a chance tearing that tender skin or banging his head. Why don't you let him go free this weekend?"

Dean and I were overjoyed. Meticulously we orchestrated the great escape. We prepared a still camera with fast film and a Camcorder to document the moment. "These may be the best shots we'll ever get of this pheasant," proclaimed Dean. We asked another neighbor, Pat, to join us and help. Each of us wore bright clothing that would look colorful against the drab hay fields. Our spot for the release was a small rise in the middle of the big field between our houses. From here Napoleon could choose the direction he wanted to fly. The pine windbreak, little woods, tall grass, and drainage ditch all offered good cover.

We had little trouble catching him that Sunday afternoon. The pheasant huddled down in my shirt, and I wrapped it closely about him. Could Napoleon sense our purpose? Slowly we walked into the field. Dean focused his telephoto lens. Pat turned on the Camcorder. "Perfect lighting. Great shadows," he breathed. "Okay, Anne, you stand on top of the rise, hold Napoleon up in your arms. Act as if you're about to toss him into the air. But don't do that. I want to take several shots."

Carefully I unwrapped the flannel shirt, dropped it to the ground, and lifted the bird over my head. A wave of nostalgia swept through me. This would be the last time I'd hold this treasured bird. Everything was still.

The sun edged behind leafless trees like a huge tangerine. Two red-winged blackbirds trilled in the distance. A porcupine clambered slowly down a maple tree, having fed on its new buds. The first robins were sweetly caroling over on Dean's front lawn.

Napoleon had had enough. With a double kick like a trained swimmer, he shot horizontally out of my arms

Holding Napoleon inside her shirt, Anne awaits the moment of his release. *Photo by: Dean Spaulding*

and flew like a jet across the field. Seconds later he was bouncing among the pine branches. The three of us raced to see if he was injured. Our last glimpse of Napoleon was a beige, light blue, cinnamon, forest green, and russet rocket streaking under the windbreak of pines.

"Darn," said Pat ruefully, "I didn't take a single foot of film."

"Gee, I'm sorry," I began, still panting. "He suddenly just took off."

"It doesn't matter," smiled Dean, "it was a super send-off. That pheasant must be ecstatic!" He opened his camera bag and dropped his Nikon in. "Come on back to the rise," he said. There he took out a bottle of champagne, three glasses, and a can of macadamia nuts. "A toast," he crowed, "to Napoleon."

We raised our bubbly glasses toward the peach-and-purple sunset. "Bye, bye, Napoleon!" we chorused. "Good luck wherever you go."

"Want to bet?" asked Dean. "I'd say our pet pheasant will be waking us up at 5:30 A.M. again in just a few days...*kok-cack, kok-cack, kok-cack.*"

12

A Mouse in My Truck

I really can't say when the mouse started living in my truck. Or whether it was a mouse from the cabin land or from my farm property. I don't know if it was a female or male, a mother or father of mouselets, how old it was, or its social security number.

What I can say for sure is it moved in about a year and a half ago and most likely came from my farmland. There's a well-built, two-car garage next to the old house. It's full of shelves, cubbyholes, cupboards, and mouse-size entrances where the overhead doors meet the concrete floor. Grass clippings frequently litter the side where the riding mower is parked. Rolls of partially used fiberglass are stacked against the wall. Plenty of newspapers are piled there for wood fires and picnics. In short, any mouse could create a comfortable, safe nest in my garage. And many did!

One summer I discovered a mouse condominium in an unused cupboard. Each of the five shelves had fluffy beds (king size) of "Pink Panther" fiberglass. And each shelf contained a family. No less than 18 mice leaped out of that cupboard the day I inadvertently yanked open its door. It was instant eviction!

Probably the truck mouse came from that condo complex. It was only a few inches to reach my vehicle, a few minutes to figure out how to scale the tires and search for a new apartment inside. Shortly after the incident in my garage, a service station attendant

A Mouse in My Truck

found a mouse nest in my air filter. He replaced the filter and admonished me to periodically check under the hood. The next nest was in the heat duct under the dash. This time I had to take my vehicle to a Chevy dealer so they could remove the entire plastic dashboard, disconnect the duct, and extract the nest. My bill was $42.00. The next nest was in early stages of construction beside the antifreeze container. It was empty, as were all the others, so I flung it aside, yet not without feeling mighty impressed by the engineering skill of that mouse.

There seemed no way to stop this daring architect. The tires and heavy steel framework under the truck provided horizontal highways to any part of the interior. I refused to trap her or him. White-tail deer mice are among the cutest of woodland mammals. They have immaculate white bellies, large alert ears, intelligent black eyes, tiny pink paws, and soft gray fur. They are as agile as monkeys and can slip through the tiniest crack or hole to find food. I love everything about these wee bandits except their black droppings which get scattered everywhere they feed.

All sorts of food is stored in my truck, year-in, year-out: Bags of dog chow, cookies, lollipops from the bank, freeze-dried camping food, and brownies. It became a game with me to see what that mouse ate for dinner each time I opened the door. Mysterious holes appeared at the bottoms of dog chow bags. Little half-moons were chewed into cookies and brownies. Shredded lollipop papers littered the floor. The mouse even nibbled the foil bags off Mountain House beef stroganoff!

When the weather turned cold and I had to turn on the heater, I often received a tiny snowstorm of tissue paper. Sometimes it was a tornado of blue carpet bits or yellow seat stuffing. Then there were blizzards of black and tan dog hairs. At least that mouse didn't plug up the heater so badly that I had to return to the

Chevy dealer.

My mouse—by now I envisioned a him and called him Timothy—became well-educated. Whenever I drive long distances to book signings, lectures, dentist or doctor appointments, airports, or camping trips, I listen to Recorded Books, Inc. (unabridged books on tape). Timothy and I went through *Typhoon* by Joseph Conrad (exciting); *The Body Farm* by Patricia Cornwall (chilling); parts of *Walden* (ho-hum, thought the mouse); WOODSWOMAN (ho-hum, said I); and *Beach Music* by Pat Conroy (too violent, we agreed).

On short trips to the post office or grocery store, we heard *All Things Considered* and *Car Talk* on public radio. Since I don't live near any amenities at the cabin (75 miles to the closest city) and have very few amenities at the farm (a small town is about 10 miles away), the radio or tape deck is always on. They truly are the "commuter's friend."

Every year I drive an average of 16,000 miles, mainly on business. During the time Timothy lived in my truck he probably racked up 25,000 miles and 35 books-on-tape. He became not only well-educated, compared to most mice, but well-travelled.

One early April day I was bound for Rochester to lecture at a large high school about my work in Guatemala on the now-extinct giant grebes. The back of my truck was loaded with a projector, slide carousels, boxes of books, a portable PA system, and lecture clothing and shoes.

Chekika and Xandor, of course, were lying on the bed in my truck camper. The mouse, I suspected, was holed up underneath them. That's where I keep a sleeping bag, pad, pillows, down jacket, camping food, wood for a fire, axe, tire chains, hiking stick, snowshoes, extra boots, and a plastic toboggan. Timothy could make himself very comfortable inside this steel box on wheels. It's a truck for all seasons.

The day was sunny, crisp, and windy. Yet as I

approached Rochester a wall of gray mounted before us. I flicked on my CB to the weather channel and listened. "Heavy lake-effect snow is expected this morning," the announcer said, "intensifying through the day. The band will spread from Lake Ontario to cover the Thruway as far east as Utica, north to Watertown, and west past Buffalo. Snow may also be expected south towards Ithaca and Binghamton."

I was due to speak at noon, so I drove on towards the wall of grey, hoping the snow would be light. The transition from bright day to snow storm was sudden and alarming. Most of the traffic slowed at once from 60 to 30 MPH. I switched on my headlights and four-way blinkers. Only the 18-wheelers kept pounding past, spraying my truck with slush. My windshield wipers were clogged with heavy flakes. The road already had two inches on it, and the snow was deepening fast. After about 20 miles through this howling blizzard, I saw an exit with phone booths and drove off the Thruway. After paying my ticket, I called the school.

The principle said worriedly, "You better not chance the drive, Anne, even though you're only 30 miles away. This storm's expected to last all day and drop eight to ten inches. We may have to close school and send the kids home."

I breathed a sigh of disappointment and relief. "Oh, I so wanted to talk to your students. But it's really scary out on the highway. I can't see a hundred feet ahead. Anyone could ram into my tailgate. Or I might hit someone creeping along in front of me."

"Don't try it," warned the principle. "We can always reschedule."

Slowly I drove back through the ticket booth and headed east towards Syracuse. The storm had intensified. I soon realized my route could not be via the Thruway or diagonally through the Adirondacks. This entire part of the state was prime lake-effect snow country. I was blocked in every direction but south.

At the first exit, I headed down toward Ithaca. After a few miles the blizzard lessened. The sun began to burn eerily through the grey scud. Nearing my old college town, I drove into blazing sun again. Cornell's proud clock tower glinted up on the hill. Yet that sinister wall of white death was pushing inexorably behind me. I stopped, quickly walked the dogs, gave them water, bought coffee and doughnuts, threw some crumbs to the mouse, and kept on trucking.

It was noon. The only way safely around the storm was to drive to Binghamton, pick up I-88 to Albany, get on the Northway (I-87) and stay on it until the exit nearest my farm. My route made two sides of an enormous triangle, covering over 350 miles. It would take over seven hours, but keep us well away from the Great Lakes. The normal route was only 200 miles and took four hours.

The dogs sensed my tension and stayed quietly on their bed. I put on a book tape—was it *Typhoon*?—and settled down to drive. Snow squalls came and went. Fierce winds buffeted the truck. The heater spewed out bits of red wool. (Where had *that* come from?) By seven o'clock we were climbing out of the Chevy at my farm. I was no richer, but I was alive! "Okay, boys, jump out," I said to Chekika and Xandor. "Okay, Timothy, you're back in your garage."

I always imagined that the mouse didn't mind my dogs. Even when they barked at passing mongrels or bounced around the camper, he was in no danger. Timothy was safe and cozy under their bed and kept riding with us for over a year.

Then last summer my Adirondack dentist found a major problem. Two old gold crowns had leaked, and the teeth beneath were badly decayed. This began a saga of dental appointments which spanned from August into February. My mileage came close to 2,000 miles, since I lived so far from professional help. An

A Mouse in My Truck

endodontist saved one tooth with a root canal; the other needed pulling.

I found an oral surgeon a hundred miles away and made an appointment. During the consultation, I told him to put me to sleep. "I'm terrified of having an extraction," I explained.

He gave me papers to read and sign, and instructions on what to wear, when to fast, and what to expect. We set a date in early November. Because I would be heavily sedated, a friend would have to drive me to her home and watch over me for 24 hours.

A complicated plan went into action. I decided to close up my cabin in late October and move to the farm in order to be closer to the oral surgeon. A drive on the Northway seemed far more tolerable than running my boat down the lake, maybe encountering ice, and driving two to three hours—all on an empty stomach.

The dogs and I left extra early on the day of my ordeal. I would drop them off at my friend's house. We were getting close to the sign that reads: LEAVING THE ADIRONDACK PARK. I always throw out a kiss and a prayer here, hoping to get back inside the Park safely and as soon as possible. I noticed some bridge repair work, a few Department of Transportation workers along the shoulder, and a DOT truck parked two miles down the road in the right lane. A huge sign with flashing yellow arrow hung from its tailgate, directing motorists to merge left.

As I slowed to 55 MPH (the speed limit was 65) in the middle lane, a white service van sped by on the right. I glimpsed two men talking busily in the front seat. They were going 70 MPH and had not yet noticed the DOT truck. With utter disbelief, I realized they were going to crash into its back end.

I moved my hand to blow the horn, hoping to startle them into attention. 'Kika was staring out the front window from her place as "co-pilot." Xandor had stuck his head through the open sliding window between camper and cab. There wasn't even time to touch the horn.

Feeling as if everything moved in slow motion, I watched with horror as the van hit the large truck, skewed sideways, and blocked the other two lanes of the Northway. It loomed directly in front of me—two seconds? one second? 100 yards? 100 feet? away.

In that last split second, I instinctively swerved hard left. The truck crashed into the guard rails at a 45-degree angle. Chekika bumped into my side. Xandor's head and neck shoved forward. There was about seven feet of clearance between the van's rear and the guard cables. Somehow I careened through that narrow opening. The cables bent, then snapped the Chevy back onto the highway. I braked and pulled across the interstate onto the far right shoulder. Instantly I checked my dogs, marvelling that they hadn't been bashed into the windshield. Instead, they whined and pawed me in confusion. "It's all right, boys," I soothed, stroking their heads.

Looking backwards I saw the entire Northway was filling up with 18-wheelers, cars, more DOT trucks, and workers running on foot. The van stood with its roof ripped off, doors flung open, its contents spilled all over the road. But no one had yet approached it. I ran toward it, thinking, I'm an EMT...I'm supposed to help. The nearer I got, the more I hesitated, afraid of what I'd find. Just then the driver's door opened and a man stumbled out. He was alive! Not even bleeding. How was it possible? Then I realized that he, too, had swerved at that final fatal micro-second. His passenger, however, was dead—without a head. The driver began screaming hysterically. He ran to the rear doors and crazily heaved the big boxes inside onto the highway so he could crawl in.

At that point, I stopped, turned around, and thought, "I can't stand to see this. It's too much."

Police sirens were keening in the distance and an ambulance was racing the wrong direction up the highway. Expert help was at hand. Back in my truck I started sobbing and shuddering. Five DOT workers walked over, tapped on the window, and motioned me out.

"Come on over to our truck. It's warm in there and we have extra coffee. You've had an awful fright," one said kindly.

Suddenly my stomach growled. I'd been fasting since 8:00 P.M. and now it was 10:00 A.M. I stumbled towards their truck. Someone opened a door for me. A woman got in from the opposite side and held out her arms. "Cry," she said. "It's the best thing you can do."

After my sobs subsided, I asked if she had anything to eat. "I'm ravenous." Then I remembered the dental appointment.

She gave me her lunch, a tasty pasta salad, and radioed out to the DOT dispatcher so a call could be made to cancel my tooth extraction.

"Thanks," I said and smiled wanly. "You saved me from a terrible 'excavation.'"

Three hours later, I'd given a signed statement to the state police as the main witness. They'd looked my truck over for damages and inspected the deeply gouged tire tracks alongside the guard rails. "Nice defensive driving," one commented. Beyond the cables, the land dropped steeply down to the northbound lane. If they'd snapped, it might have meant another death.

Slowly, somberly, I drove to my friend's home. I noted the drag from my left tire and guessed it was badly out of line. She was waiting nervously, fearing an accident had delayed me. We sat down at a table. Quietly I murmured, "Life is so damn fragile. It can end in a fraction of a second. Human error is all it takes."

"The dogs?" she began.

"Okay, thank God. Without seat belts on them or air bags, they could have been killed instantly. Oh, and I might have lost Timothy."

My friend looked at me quizzically. "Timothy? Who's that?"

"My mouse," I said shyly. "The one that lives in the truck."

November, December, and January raged full of snow storms and high winds. How I hated and feared driving. I was constantly changing dental appointments to avoid slippery roads. Or maybe I was avoiding the 'excavation,' yet it was finally pulled. One brilliant February afternoon, too cold to go walking, I decided to take the truck out of the garage and drive down the dirt road so that Chekika and Xandor could run.

As I neared the intersection, a very tall man walking a very small Schnauzer came toward me. I stopped the truck and ordered both dogs to jump into the camper. Yet the minute they were inside, they saw the little dog and began barking furiously and dashing from window to window.

Just to add to the confusion, my neighbor, Dean, drove up behind me and stopped. Now Xandor wanted to get out and greet him. Whining, he scratched at the tailgate. The Schnauzer scrabbled with its paws at the truck door and yapped shrilly. I jumped out. Three people and three dogs were noisily milling around on a road that generally didn't see traffic between 8:00 A.M. and 5:00 P.M.

A high-speed crash had not fazed Timothy, but this time it was too much. The noise, the doors opening and closing, the scratching down low, close to his nest, the odor of a strange dog...he leapt onto the hard cold road. Looked this way and that. Zigged one way, zagged the other. Then he came back to the rear tire and put his tiny pink paws on the black rubber wall. He looked up beseechingly, black eyes popping. Dean and I stared in astonishment. It was my first look at Timothy.

"It's my mouse!" I cried. "He wants to go back inside."

"Back in your truck?" asked Dean amazed.

Before I could answer, Timothy ran under the truck and over the snowy shoulder and disappeared among some rocks and grass. Gone.

I waved goodbye to the tall man, said "so long" to Dean, and hushed my dogs. I turned the truck around and parked it next to the mouse's paw prints. We waited quietly—first with the motor running, then without. No mouse came back.

At last I had to go. Crumbling up some cookies and bits of brownie, I scattered them among the rocks. Timothy would find some supper that way. But my heart sank. This was the coldest snap of the winter, due to drop to $-20°F$ that night. A stabbing north wind blew. It was a quarter of a mile back to the garage.

Could the mouse smell home? Would he return? Or might he try to knit together a nest from the grass and curl up under a rock? Could he freeze to death? If he ran home at night, a great horned owl might spot him—such a plump, shiny, delectable tidbit. If he ran home by day, a shrike or the goshawk could pick him off.

That night I parked my truck in its usual spot in the garage. I left some pumpkin cake outside the overhead door. Inside, I set a cookie on the truck seat, a lollipop on the floor, and a dog biscuit on the camper bed. Offerings from his friends.

Sliding the overhead door down, I paused a moment to watch Venus hanging brilliantly above the frozen farm pond. Saturn shone at her side, reddish, remote, and steady. I reflected on how Timothy had been making his way along with me in a technological world for such a long time. He was using my steel box on wheels as his condo, cafeteria, and safehouse. We'd managed to go around Nature's storms and man's accidents by the skin of our teeth. But when human chaos set in, the mouse tried to hang on, then simply said, "The hell with you," and left.

Sometimes I'd like to do the same exact thing—leave my steel box on wheels. Go back to the cabin full-time and make my entire living inside my log box deep in the old-growth forest. Get away from fearsome highways and scary storms. But I need technology to make a living, so I have to stay in that precarious world full of people. And now I'd have to go on alone.

In the morning most of the cake outside was gone. But it could have been Xandor, or wild mice, ravens, or even coyotes. The cookies, lollipop, and biscuit were untouched inside.

I miss the mouse in my truck. I was sorry to see him go. I'm still waiting and wishing for Timothy to come home.

13

Puppy Xandor

My farm pond was exceptionally quiet. I stopped pruning the apple trees just below its berm, and listened intently. The April afternoon was windless. A robin's-egg-blue sky arched benignly over the ice-covered pond. Thin as this ice was, I heard no creaking or cracking. No melt-water trickled down the overflow pipe. *Where* was that puppy?

Five minutes earlier Chekika, Puppy Xandor, and I had walked from farmhouse to pond. The spring sun shone strong and made pools of melted water on the surface. Around the pond's edges, bedraggled cattails stood in a sliver of open water. Yet the ice sheet was still thick enough to support the three of us. My wise older female and the little pup ventured farther onto the gray granular sheet to explore. It was the first time he had ever seen ice.

An uneasy feeling crept up my back. A sixth sense urged me to climb the berm and check the pond. Chekika was on the far shore, sniffing snowshoe hare tracks in a remnant patch of snow. Xandor was nowhere to be seen. Suddenly, I noticed a small animal clinging to an ice floe, body submerged in freezing water. Only the head and big ears stuck out. Without a whimper, the puppy flailed weakly at the floe. It was plain to see he'd wandered too close to the overflow pipe where the honey-combed ice was thinnest and plunged through. By now, I estimated, he'd been in that frigid water for three minutes.

Xandor looked at me pathetically. In a minute or two he would weaken, grow numb, and slide to the bottom. I'd have never found him until summer. The horrible vision of locating that tiny black corpse with its thin red collar, on the pond bottom, using face mask and flippers, flashed through my mind.

Instantly, I leaped onto the ice, letting my knees and hands take my weight, spread-eagling across its rotten surface. I grabbed for Xandor's red collar and pulled the puppy toward me. Then, with a sick slushy sound, the ice caved in, and I fell forward into four and a half feet of 33°F water. My head and arms went under. I dragged Puppy Xandor down with me. He struggled desperately. Fighting to get my boots onto the bottom, I pushed my shoulders and the dog upward. Abruptly we broke back into the dazzling spring light. In that micro-second of dizzy shock, the sun spun like a huge firecracker sparkling and wheeling in the sky.

Feet secure, I held his little head above water and surged through the soggy ice. My work-worn Carhart padded pants and wool jacket kept some of the steely cold from my body. Yet in my panic, I never even felt the numbing cold. One more violent shove, and I waded onto shore with the puppy in my arms.

Immediately, I stripped off wet clothes and boots. Standing stark naked on the lawn, I streaked for the farmhouse with the puppy scampering behind. Inside I toweled Xandor and myself dry. I wrapped him in a quilted flannel shirt and put on a dry outfit. Out on the sheltered back porch, I laid him down on the sunny floor and curled up around the puppy. I held him tight to my belly and chest to share body heat. Then I waited to see if he would succumb to hypothermia. Luckily the run and the sun did wonders. His circulation and mine renewed almost at once. Puppy Xandor fell asleep as I cuddled him. Then I began to cry.

I cried for the swiftness and cruelness which is part

Puppy Xandor

of Death. I wept because this new, bright, happy little ball of life, only ten weeks old, almost got snatched away. I'd just arrived home with him from Arizona the day before. What a traumatic home-coming for a puppy—from desert heat to icy pond. Eventually I quieted and dozed.

When Puppy Xandor woke up, he seemed sobered and subdued. I smothered him in blankets and tucked him inside the airline kennel which he had accepted as "bed." Then I went to finish my pruning, to pull out some maple taps and buckets of sap, and to find Chekika.

One week ago I had found this beguiling puppy alone in a huge cage, fragrant with cedar shavings, at a kennel in Tucson. Intelligence and curiosity glowed from his chestnut eyes. One ear was up; the other down. His jet-black muzzle, head, and back contrasted boldly with his raised golden "eyebrows," broad chest,

Newly arrived from Arizona, Puppy Xandor nestles in Anne's arms on back porch of the farm.

and strong legs. He was the last of a litter. He looked lonesome—and handsome.

At the urging of a good friend, Lucy, who also owns and loves shepherds, I'd flown to Arizona to inspect the new spring litters at this immaculate kennel. Unfortunately, all the litters were too young for me to make a sensible choice. They were still squiggly, blind, suckling babies attached to their mothers' teats. I needed an older puppy, and it would have a lot to live up to. But I felt the ten-week-old one was too old. Eight weeks is the ideal age.

Chekika and I had mourned for Condor one long year. We had moped about the farm in winter and gazed nostalgically around the cabin at his favorite haunts in summer. 'Kika needed a frisky companion to coax her into play again. I needed a smart, assertive protector who would love the woods and make our "pack" complete again.

The owner talked on, but I sensed she was subtly pressuring me. "Let's go to lunch and talk it over," I suggested to my friend, as I backed away.

Over huge spinach salads and Arizona iced tea, Lucy told me, "I think this kennel really has good genetic lines. That's very hard to find in America and Canada today, Anne. Too many 'puppy mills' are passing along inferior genes. You should always check if the parents are certified by the Orthopedic Foundation for Animals, or OFA." She went on to explain, "They are working to reduce the frequency of hip dysplasia. Thanks to them there's been a decrease in this condition in German shepherds of 10 to 20 percent in the past few years, and a similar decrease in many other breeds. Your best bet, if you don't like this puppy, is to go to eastern Germany or Czechoslovakia where there are still clean lines of working shepherds."

I grimaced. How could I possibly manage to leave my work and do that, much less afford it? Already I'd looked around local New York kennels without success.

Puppy Xandor

Now I began to feel a sense of urgency. Lucy was going on vacation at the end of the week. I had to fly home before Easter rush. I would have to decide today. Fiddling with my sweating glass of iced tea, I brooded.

"Spring is the perfect time for a new puppy," Lucy reminded me, licking a spoon of tamarind sherbet. "Let's go check out a couple of other kennels so you can compare what's available. Maybe that will help you decide."

We stopped for gas. I begged to pay since my hostess was being so kind and helpful. The attendant gave me three shiny new pennies in change. A good sign!

The other kennels and litters didn't begin to measure up to the first. One was filthy. The bitches in others displayed lackluster coats, poor conformation, or were skin and bones. We went back to see the ten-week-old pup. He gazed longingly at me through the chain link fence. The breeder placed him on a thin leash and told me to walk around with the puppy. He followed eagerly. Clearly he was ready to go home with me. Then he put huge front paws on my leg and tried to lick my face. I was smitten.

The kennel owner gave me the pedigrees, bill of sale, instructions for worming and feeding, the leash, a brush, and a contract guaranteeing good health and breeding, with the clause stating that if I was not satisfied with the dog within the first two years, it could be returned.

As I wrote out my check, I noted the date was 3/31/93. Three more threes. Another good sign!

Lastly, there was the puppy's name. "Zandor" was his great grandfather's registered name. It sounded rather like Condor. I liked that. Only I changed the Z to X. Z sounded like Zorro, the Fox. X made it more elegant—almost like Alexander the Great.

All this ran through my mind as I worked steadily on my farm that April afternoon. I stopped often to inspect Xandor, making sure he was warm. Each time he awoke and smothered my face with licks. I smiled affectionately at him. How could I know that this near-drowning was only the first of many death-defying acts that Puppy Xandor would engage in during his youth?

Actually, his splashy, flashy life style started right in Tucson. After buying him, I picked up a large airline kennel which would become his "safe house." That first day he adopted it. The second, he became housebroken. The trick, I found, was to let him outdoors immediately after meals and when he woke at night. He slept exactly six hours at a stretch, waking at midnight and at first bird call. Then he whined and scratched like a cougar. His nighttime sorties made me very nervous. Coyotes chorused up the canyon. Great horned owls hooted on the hills. They might relish this 20-pound scrap of tender meat. Also rattlers and scorpions were out hunting, and I feared their bite or sting might kill a small puppy.

On our third day together, my friend said goodbye and left me her Mercedes-Benz to use until I flew back east. So that afternoon Puppy Xandor and I drove up Mt. Lemmon in grand style. He adjusted well from 85°F heat to snow drifts atop that 10,000-foot peak. The puppy adored pouncing at his shadow on the snow and gobbling the white stuff like a frosty milkshake.

"You'll be right at home in the Adirondacks," I assured him.

The fourth day we visited Saguaro National Monument. By mid-morning temperature was in the eighties again and Xandor's black coat was absorbing every bit of heat. We rested under a mesquite tree, but when I started walking again the puppy stayed down and looked at me pitifully. "Don't make me walk anymore," he seemed to be saying.

Turning him over to see if he was hurt, I noted his huge puppy paws were as pink and soft as a baby's feet. Astonished, I realized he'd never been away from the kennel, rarely out of his cage there, and had never

Puppy Xandor

walked a trail. I picked him up and continued along the Desert Ecology Trail. The sun felt like a blowtorch on my skin. The distant Rincon Mountains shimmered and trembled in the heat waves. I imagined how Xandor felt in his fur coat. Suddenly, he began to hyperventilate.

Hurriedly, I rushed back to the locked and now broiling Mercedes. I started the engine and turned on the air conditioner which was turned down to 62 degrees. Nothing happened. Quickly, I rolled down all the windows and started driving through the park, hoping the breeze would cool the puppy. He lay prostrate on the front seat, panting terribly fast. Stories of dogs heat-stroking-out in 15 minutes flickered through my brain. But how to cool him down?

Around the next bend I saw a small shallow stream spilling over the roadway. It was probably snow melt-water trickling down from the Rincons. A godsend! Screeching to a stop, I dragged Puppy Xandor into the creek and splashed water all over him. It was cool and clear. Soon he recovered. Now the breeze wicked away moisture and helped cool him more.

The sixth day was our flight back to New York. Lucy had arranged for a cab to pick me up at 5:00 A.M. I was ready long before dawn, with the dog crate and my luggage down by the drive and the puppy on his leash. As we waited for transportation to arrive, a melon-orange glow crept up the canyon and the first cactus wrens began caroling. The desert air was cool and fragrant. I hated to leave this sunny, brilliant land. Back in New York there might still be lingering ice and snow.

Twin lights picked their way slowly up the winding road. At last, I thought, the cab. My plane left at 7:00 A.M. and I still had to check the air kennel in ahead of myself. Xandor and I would be on the same flight. A gray stretch limo glided to a stop next to me. A uniformed driver stepped out. Gray leather seats, a color TV, and bar with fancy decanters met my stare. The driver spoke my name. "Ready?" he asked. Had my friend made a mistake? Had she done this for a joke, knowing I drive a pickup truck? Had she planned it as a gift? Or what?

There was no time to wonder, for now Xandor's cage would not fit into the trunk. The driver had to slide it onto the front seat. The puppy and I rode elegantly in back while the chauffeur maintained a stony silence. Once he said sternly, "Don't let him pee on the floor!"

At 6:30 A.M., Xandor disappeared down the American Airlines luggage ramp. I fought back tears. Stories of oxygen, pressure, and heat failures in the cargo hold gripped me. At best, the six or seven hours trip seemed a long time for a tiny pup to be confined. I tried to get hold of myself.

In Chicago, a helpful gate attendant actually opened the door and allowed me to go down to the plane. Two burly cargo men were just lifting out the air kennel. Xandor was peering at me brightly. I opened the cage, offered food and water, then walked him around the tarmac on his red leash. The puppy ceremoniously squatted to pee, dwarfed by the huge 757 tire.

A change of planes in Chicago, and then we were back in Albany by nightfall. Cage and puppy came trundling along the noisy luggage ramp. I swiftly lifted them off and opened the door. Passengers everywhere stooped to pet Puppy Xandor and admire him. He made lots of people happy. I was so excited to be safely back that I forgot my luggage. Next morning I went back to the airport to pick it up and then headed for the farm.

Chekika, however, was not happy when I picked her up en route at a boarding kennel. She smelled another dog all over me. Instead of her usual prancing, barking, licking, and wiggling, she was subdued. She looked older. I noticed the pinched look around her muzzle, her downcast eyes and slinking walk. She was jealous!

Even after she saw and smelled that cunning black ball of fur, she didn't relent. At once, I resolved to treat her as #1 Dog in our new pack. She would always eat first, drink first, get treats first, be cuddled first, and sleep next to my bed every night.

Chekika's jealous streak lasted all April. She either ignored Xandor or growled menacingly at him with teeth showing. I wondered if I'd made a major mistake bringing such a young dog into her staid, stable, sad life. After all, she was the equivalent of 60 years old in human terms and deserved a bit of peace and quiet.

In May I had to leave for four days to lecture and do book signings in western New York. I put both dogs into my favorite kennel. The owner wisely separately the two. Xandor played for hours in a run with Maggie, a yellow lab puppy. Chekika wandered freely about the office and storage room. She was the official "office dog" and greeted every new boarder and its owner. At night she slept snugly beside bags of dog chow and cat litter in the storeroom where it was quiet. Everyone who passed gave her a pet and a kind word.

When I picked 'Kika up this time, she looked younger. She was pleased to see me, and even greeted the puppy half-heartedly. All the attention at the kennel had apparently soothed her ruffled feelings. Moreover, Puppy Xandor had gained weight, and was stronger and more playful. Now the two could play hide-and-seek or tag, or she could bowl him over and over in the lush green grass. Clearly, she was the alpha dog.

Lucy was now in the Adirondacks, so I went to see my Arizona friend and show off Puppy Xandor. He was dressed up with red ribbons and beige lace streamers tied to his red collar. His nails shone shiny black on those huge paws, and his teeth were a gleaming white and beautifully shaped. His stance was classic shepherd. As Xandor tumbled out of my truck, an enormous eight-month old female Rottweiler raced around the corner of the house toward him.

Puppy Xandor panicked and began bawling in terror. He raced toward the front porch and wedged himself into a small space under the boards. The Rottweiler panted and pawed at him, eager to play. I was still beside the truck. Lucy was at her front door. Xandor had no other place to hide. Suddenly, Chekika lunged at the huge dog with terrible snarls and snaps of her fangs. A tangled mass of black, brown, and fawn-colored hair rolled across the lawn. Although a third smaller than the Rottweiler, 'Kika gave her a thrashing and sent her running. She was protecting *her puppy!*

At length, Puppy Xandor was pried out of his hideyhole. Lucy and I tried to calm him down. But it was clear our visit was over before it began, so shaken was the little dog. I piled both him and Chekika into the truck and drove home. Xandor sat meekly on the front seat, leaning against Chekika, ears at half mast. The cheery red and beige streamers were smeared with mud. 'Kika's fur was streaked with spittle. They acted like two kids who'd gotten in a fight at school and missed a birthday party.

From then on, the two formed a fast friendship. I often reinforced our pack status by sleeping on the floor with them—beside the wood stove at the farm, outdoors at the cabin, or in a tent. Traveling by boat or canoe, I raised a special golf umbrella above them when it rained hard, since they didn't like to get wet. In the truck, they both laid on the bed in the camper and put their heads through the cab rear window to stare at the roadway. Loved? Spoiled? You bet your life. Yet they were far more than just pets. We shared friendship, protection, fun, adventure, and affection.

Puppy Xandor turned out to be just the opposite of Condor. In contrast to the serious, austere demeanor and calm, graceful gait of my former shepherd, Xandor's personality was buoyant and lovable, his pace that of a charging buffalo. He would bump into my legs, careen against trees and furniture, leap up on truck doors, and step on my toes or anything else lying

Chekika and Xandor travel on a bed in the truck cap, peering out its sliding window at roadway.

In heavy rains, Chekika and Xandor like to keep dry under a giant golf umbrella in the boat.

on the floor. He was an adorable, clumsy clown.

By now, the ice was out of Black Bear Lake and the forest was turning green. It was high time to introduce Xandor to my cabin. And, sure enough, a whole new set of death-defying adventures was about to begin.

14

Mr. Xandor

On the vibrant spring day we headed back to open camp, it didn't take Puppy Xandor long to learn about boats. My 14-foot Alumacraft was piled high with files, boxes of books, dog food, building supplies, guiding gear, and a luxurious five-foot-wide Boston fern. I coaxed the little pup over the gunwhale. He bleated nervously a few times, glancing often at Chekika for reassurance. She was posing imperturbably as bowsprit.

I placed Xandor between my legs, tickled his tummy, and praised him. Slowly I started the motor. He tried to leap out, away from the throbbing sound. I let the motor idle and repeated the process with Xandor. Gradually, he calmed down. I eased the engine into forward and started up the lake.

Puppy Xandor watched with amazement as we passed our resident pair of loons, who chorused, a flotilla of young mergansers wobbling over the surface, and tree reflections that pushed into wavy disorder. His antenna ears and saucer-like eyes absorbed every aspect of this mysterious voyage.

At last we rounded the rocky point and tied up at my dock. Xandor had a tantalizing new place to investigate. Frogs, red squirrels, robins, chipmunks, garter snakes, beavers, and ravens vied for his attention. He scrambled after 'Kika and me to the cabin. Inside it was full of my smell, Chekika's odor, and more faintly the scent of another male shepherd. He found old chewed cow hooves, stuffed toys, and rawhide bones waiting to be attacked. A big red pail holding cold lake water and a dog biscuit let him know this was a great place for snacks. Finally, he loped out with us to inspect a strange, three-sided lean-to, a woodshed redolent with yellow birch logs and chainsaw mix, and a tiny square building that reeked of human droppings (*he* thought).

Within that first week, Puppy Xandor survived three close calls. The first time, a new rabies tag on his choke collar slipped between the dock boards and got caught. The little dog was pinned down, struggling to get to his feet, and almost suffocating. The uneasy silence of "No Xandor Around" alerted me. Quickly I made a search and freed him.

The next emergency was a stout twig he'd chewed off a branch. It became lodged crosswise in his upper jaws. He raced to the cabin, flailing his head from side to side and grunting with frustration. He sat beside me, pawing frantically. I spoke sharply to him, plunged my hand in his mouth, and pried the twig out.

Another afternoon he ran under a large fallen tree, stubbed his forehead on a dead branch, and fell down. Lying half-unconscious, he squeaked piteously. Then he stood up and stumbled toward me. Fearful of a concussion, I immediately pulled him into the lake and doused his head with cold water. After a few minutes of quiet cuddling and cold compresses, Puppy Xandor revived.

The dogs' biggest problem was black flies. They emerged in full vigor and hunger to discover the tender, pink, enormous ears of both shepherds. I had to smear Old Woodsman repellent on them every couple hours. They hated the tarry smell (*I* love it). But gradually we three became sluggish from blackfly venom.

My super project for 1993 was to construct a tiny office way back on my land. My writing profession now demanded a phone machine, fax, and photocopier to enhance book distribution and communication with editors and publishers. The building was a prodigious undertaking. For starters, my hired helpers had to carry a prefabed storage shed on their backs more than 1,000 feet through a pathless woods. We had to figure out a simple, durable foundation we could lay without digging holes and pouring concrete. There were packs of heavy asphalt shingles to manhandle to the site. And, finally, all carpentry had to be done with handtools. The advertising panel stated: "Two men, two days, two tools." Poppycock! It took weeks.

Puppy Xandor loved the hustle and bustle of construction. While Chekika dozed sensibly under a shady, bushy balsam, the pup had to check out everything. He tried to eat staples. He chewed hammer handles. He munched sandpaper. He was unfazed by chainsaws and stood right next to them. Fearing for his safety and deafness, I yelled myself hoarse telling him, "Go!"

One hot afternoon we were shingling the roof. Xandor lay panting on cool, fresh earth at the base of the shed. All at once a carpenter's large metal square slid off the roof and plunged into the dirt right next to Xandor's head. Never had I owned a shepherd so accident-prone!

Despite the early summer heat, Puppy Xandor would *not* go into the water. Some instinctual memory warned him it was dangerous. Yet it was imperative that I train him, as I'd done with my four shepherds before, to be a water dog. They needed to feel comfortable around lakes, rivers, and assorted watercraft, so I could take them on guiding trips, go camping along lakeshores, and be sure they could save me and themselves. This training was essential.

Strangely, Xandor didn't find canoeing threatening. Safely seated in front of me on the canoe's flat bottom, the puppy was tied to the center of a thwart so he couldn't leap out. Chekika sat directly in the bow serving as an unflappable role model. The pup took to canoeing after three sessions. It brought him new animals to see and smell without the awful roar of the motorboat.

July 4th was a sultry weekend. Chekika and I spent most of our time in the water. I floated around in a rubber raft, reading and sunbathing. 'Kika chased sticks and brought them to shore. She and I swam out, then I let her pull me in with her tail. She received high praise for this life-saving trick—and a cookie. But no amount of cajoling or cookies could persuade Puppy Xandor to join us. I donned my face mask and fins to check out the dock's flotation and set a heavy cement block on the water line. Xandor watched quizzically from beneath a young pine as I disappeared underwater. Each time, he let out a whine. He stared apprehensively as if afraid I'd gone away permanently. The minute I popped to the surface the puppy let out a ragged, joyful bark.

These were his first barks, and I could sense the rapid maturation my puppy was undergoing. Having raised several shepherds, I could read the signs and predict the progress as clearly as if I were raising a child after studying the work of Piaget (the famous educational psychologist), with his chronology of human childhood development. Dogs have their own schedule of behavioral changes. They have to be trained at the right time in some areas; in others, change is instinctive.

Mid-July continued scorching. One evening the pup began hyperventilating, just as he'd done in the Arizona desert. I put a block of ice on his belly, rubbed his head and ears with ice water, and let him chew ice cubes. He recovered in about 20 minutes. It seemed to me this dog had a thermostat problem. How could he have survived being raised in Tucson? Probably he'd be dead by now of heat stroke had he stayed there.

This medical crisis served Xandor well, for shortly afterwards, he put one tentative paw in the water.

Chekika cavorted in the shallows before him. Next thing I knew, he was swimming after her. This was the start of his love of lakes. His fear was gone, and he'd come full circle from the baptism in my icy pond.

At age seven months, he weighed seventy pounds. His head was huge with a broad forehead, mischievous eyes, big black nose, and deep jowls with lips as soft as black velvet. Imagine my consternation, the first time Puppy Xandor saw a baby lying among towels on a friend's dock. Because he was so big, the parents might consider him threatening. Before I could grab his collar (now many sizes larger than the first), he had gamboled up to the infant and licked its naked face and body several times. The family watched spellbound. Then he frisked off to chase yellow swallowtails fluttering above yellow dandelions on their lawn. A sigh escaped from my lips. How lucky I was to own an affectionate and happy-go-lucky dog. Who cared if he was a klutz and a clown?

Mr. Xandor, one year old, with his first Easter bunny.

Meanwhile, Xandor had been practicing his bark on umbrellas, vacuum cleaners, beavers at the cabin, and cows at the farm. It was getting deeper and more powerful. Soon it would strike fear into anyone out to harm us. And, soon, it did. One day while shopping in the city I stopped at a major intersection. Both dogs were seated on the front seat beside me. Another truck pulled up to our side with two workmen in it. The closest one leaned over, saw the two dogs, smiled and said "Wuff-Wuff." A low, menacing growl and penetrating bark filled the cab. The two men looked astonished at my puppy, then sped ahead as the red light changed. Puppy Xandor wasn't a puppy any longer. He was protecting me. He was *Mr.* Xandor!

In September he was eight months old and weighed 80 pounds. He took to lifting his leg to pee rather than squat. The cunning little cluster of hairs on his penis sheath had served him well during puppyhood by directing his urine stream downward. But recently they'd been replaced by a beige fur covering. It was now up to Xandor to direct his urine as high as he could into trees, bushes, posts, and tires. This is the way male dogs and wolves have marked their territories for eons. Luckily, I didn't need to carry on toilet training. Nature has arranged it wonderfully for her creatures, and none of my shepherds has ever left a mess near cabin or farmhouse. They are fastidious to a fault.

Mr. Xandor started helping Chekika carry my mail from the mail boat to the cabin, holding the mail bag jauntily in his jaws. Four of my shepherds had mastered the mail routine through coercion and cookies. Mail communication is one of the most important parts of my life, making a living as a freelancer, so I had to train and trust them to do it.

That fall I was asked to perform a literary reading at Lake George. I decided to bring both dogs on stage when I read the chapter about Chekika. This would be Mr. Xandor's debut. 'Kika sat primly beside me, freshly bathed, brushed, and well-mannered in her pink bandana. She obviously knew I was talking about her.

Xandor fidgeted. *He* wasn't the center of attention, although he glowed sleekly with good health and wore

Chekika leaps at a garden hose, catching the water stream in her mouth.

Snowballs don't faze Chekika. She lets them "explode" in her mouth.

a bright red bandana. Suddenly he turned and grabbed Chekika's ruff with a mock play-growl. She turned her flank and neatly pushed him away. The audience broke up. I stopped reading because it was exactly what Condor had done to Chekika eight years ago at a similar reading. "What goes around, comes around," I thought.

By winter, we were back at the farm. Days were short. Winds blew frigid. Exercise was limited. The dogs seemed bored. Normally we kept active with cross-country skiing or hikes across the dreary landscape. However, a bad bout of flu had me bed-ridden for three days and then creeping about the house with a deep cough. Xandor and 'Kika were bursting with energy, so at last I took my truck out of the garage. By running the heater until it was 70 degrees in the cab, I dared to bundle up and take them for a run down the dead-end road every day. At the end, I parked by a hay field and listened to public radio while the dogs tracked hares and played in the snowdrifts. Then, I'd drive home. The hour's outing gave them a two-mile jog and me a break from bed.

Yet after a week of his running along the stone-hard road, I noticed Xandor was limping. I checked for snow packed between his toes or cuts on his pads. Nothing. He hadn't slipped on any ice. Finally I called the vet and arranged to have him examined. Xandor was just a year old so she recommended his hips be x-rayed. It was prudent timing to check for dysplasia (a congenital hip malformation). If I wanted to breed him, I'd need X-ray proof for certifying him with the Orthopedic Foundation for Animals (OFA). Potential buyers would want to know their new puppy's sire was healthy. And so did I for Xandor's sake.

To take the films, my dog would be asleep so that his bones could be manipulated. Like any mother or devoted pet owner I felt very apprehensive about having my dog anaesthetized. Even with the vet's assurance that she'd never lost a patient to this procedure, I was scared. It was too reminiscent of when Condor was put to sleep—permanently.

So I planned to sit in the waiting room all morning, expecting to get an update on his condition from time to time, and be there when he awoke to carry him to the truck. The vet started the procedure at 9:30 A.M. Not 20 minutes had gone by when she hurried into the waiting room in her lead-shielded apron and gravely announced, "Your dog is severely dysplastic in his left hip, and starting it in his right along with arthritis."

That bombshell rooted me to the chair. I looked at her in disbelief. "Come on back. I'll show you the X rays," she volunteered.

I stared in silence as she pointed out the shallow hip sockets, and the heads of the femurs (thigh bones) sitting so poorly in these sockets, the edging of white which meant arthritis.

"But he's only a year old," I mumbled.

"True, but his genes are lousy," she said bluntly. "You should never breed him. It's not right to grow puppies if they may limp later from hip problems."

A part of my future world collapsed. I had planned on getting a female puppy from Xandor, just as I'd been blessed with Chekika from Condor. Instead, my new dog might face a restricted life with pain and increasing stiffness as he aged.

The good vet went over all the palliatives, from aspirin to Adequan to Glyco-flex (a sea mussel extract), to...I grew faint at the choices, none of which would cure the problem or stop this scourge that afflicts shepherds all over the world. Then, as an afterthought, she added, "Of course, there's hip replacement surgery."

My head snapped up. "Hip replacement? For dogs?"

"Yes. It's quite successful, but very expensive."

At once, I interrupted. "Cost is not the issue. It's the

quality of the dog's life. The pain. The immobility. If you love someone or something, you give it the best care available."

The vet looked at me sympathetically. "Then you better start saving for a hip replacement. They run between a thousand to two thousand dollars. I'm sure the Cornell Vet Hospital can do it when Xandor becomes lame. Probably when he's five or six years old."

Tenderly, I drove my woozy dog home and carried him inside next to the wood stove. Laying his head in my lap, I stroked him a long time. I just couldn't accept that such a blithe spirit, such a gorgeous creature, was going to suffer due to poor breeding.

Tentatively, a thought edged into my mind. Hadn't my contract from the kennel in Arizona said the pup would be generally free of genetic disorders? Hadn't I paid enough to ensure this? What had gone wrong? Was he a throwback? Then I recalled a clause that read: "If not satisfied with your animal, it can be returned within two years for a replacement."

A preposterous idea! What kind of an owner would do that? I'd come to love Xandor too much to part with him, to trade him. Besides, what would become of him back in that kennel? Who would ever buy a grown dog with dysplasia? Xandor would be sitting back in a big cage, full of fresh cedar shavings, looking longingly at every customer who passed him by.

All winter I stewed over his diagnosis and future. He still bounded exuberantly along cross-country ski trails and continued his funny, bungling approach to life. "Ah, you're a bamboozle, a big buffalo," I chided him affectionately. But I didn't let him run on the hard road anymore. He stopped limping.

Sometime in March the solution came clear to me. I had enough airline miles for a free ticket anywhere in the United States. So I went back to Tucson and the kennel. This was not to be a confrontation with the owner; rather, a negotiation. She needed to know about the inferior genetic outcome of her breeding program to spare future such offspring. I needed help with Xandor. I went armed with a thick scrapbook full of pictures of Puppy Xandor, his X rays, and the vet's diagnosis.

Back at that gleaming cluster of metal cages, surrounded by green lawn, with tall cacti in the distance, I asked her to sit down with me for a few moments. I showed her the photos. She was impressed with Xandor's appearance. "What a great dog," she commented.

"Well," I said, closing the scrapbook and pulling out the X rays, "there's a problem."

She examined the films and read the diagnosis. Her face darkened. Her attitude changed abruptly from friendly to defensive. "I can't explain how dysplasia got into that line," she said. "Sometimes bad recessive genes just appear. What do you want to do about it?"

Before I could reply, she went on, "You could send back the dog. Ship him by air. Our contract promises to replace any animal you're not satisfied with."

"Yes, I'm aware of that," I responded politely. "But what would happen to Xandor if he came back here?" I asked in a troubled voice. "Could you find another owner?"

The sinister truth came out. "He'd be euthanized."

Her statement, the worry, my long flight, the strain all winter suddenly overwhelmed me and I began sobbing. "But I *love* Xandor. I want to make him better. He deserves the best. He didn't ask for bad hips," I choked out. "How could I knowingly allow him to be killed?"

"You have no right to perpetuate his bad genes," said the woman matter-of-factly. "You should have him neutered at the very least."

"He'll still be in pain eventually," I said.

"What is it you want then?" she asked with a touch of exasperation. Her attention was on a rangy, black shepherd being taught attack positions. The man with him was dressed in a thick padded suit and helmet. My next words swiveled her head around.

"I'd like you to go fifty-fifty with me in the cost of a hip replacement. It's only fair. You bred Xandor and I'm his 'mother'. We are both responsible for him."

Her startled eyes stared at me in astonishment. "Why, if I did that with every customer who had a problem with her dog, I'd go broke."

Quickly I gained control of myself. This was one cool individual I was dealing with. "Look, the cost of a hip replacement will probably be around fifteen hundred dollars. Divide that in half and it's exactly the cost of another puppy replacement. Xandor's price was seven hundred and fifty, if you'll recall."

"I can't do that," she stated flatly. Our silence was broken only by the snarls and grunts of the rangy shepherd grabbing its would-be assailant's sleeve and shaking vigorously.

Something in my face must have softened the owner's attitude. She sighed, "It's nice to see a person so attached and concerned about her pet. Why don't I just give you another puppy now at half price? Take it back with you to New York."

"Thanks, but no thanks," I muttered. "I couldn't manage with three. My cabin's very small. It would become too expensive when I travel on business and have to leave them in a kennel. Besides, I'm committed to a hip replacement."

Then, from out of that blazing desert scenery, the solution came to me. "Let's do this," I suggested. "I'll keep an eye on Xandor and when he needs the operation we'll go to the Cornell Veterinary Hospital. I'll pay for it all." I shifted on the bench and took a deep breath. "Meanwhile, Chekika, my female, won't live forever. She's almost ten. Could you possibly give me a little female puppy after she dies?"

The breeder hesitated, then nodded. "Okay," she

agreed. "That'll be in two or three years, no doubt. I'll pick a nice one for you." Handing the X rays and diagnosis back to me, she said, "Now, if you'll excuse me, I have to speak to that man training the police dog. He's not doing it right." And she started to stride away.

"Wait, please," I called out. "Could you write our agreement on Xandor's contract and sign your name? I have it right here."

I caught a glint of something close to anger in her eyes as she turned back and scrawled a few words on the contract. Then she said goodbye and vanished. I gathered my things, walked to my rental car, got in, and drove away. Pensively I gazed back at the big sign of that immaculate kennel in my rear-view mirror. Was it a puppy mill? Was she a con artist? Or were the lines clean and a single flaw had just happened to appear in my dog? Had his breeding been impeccable?

High over the Arizona desert next day, I felt elated. The problem of replacing my beloved 'Kika (to avoid another bout of grief and depression) was solved. I would save $750. Yet I also felt sad. I was back where I'd started with Mr. Xandor and his problem. How bad his dysplasia might be, only time would tell.

15

An Extraordinary Summer

The spring and summer of 1992 were hot and exciting. They marked the 100th anniversary of the Adirondack Park. All kinds of events were planned, from formal dances with the New York State Forest Rangers force to academic panels on the Park's future to town barbecues. Governor Mario Cuomo traveled to Blue Mountain Lake, the heart of the Park, to present a stirring speech on May 20, the anniversary of the signing of the state law that created the park in 1892.

A year earlier I'd planned to create my own celebration. It would highlight an extraordinary New Yorker, Verplanck Colvin. It would give thanks for his extraordinary gift to New Yorkers. If it hadn't been for Colvin, I'd probably still be in New Jersey. I wouldn't be living in a log cabin by a lake. There wouldn't be wilderness tracts to guide in. In fact, there'd be *no* Adirondack Park for anyone to enjoy.

To carry out the celebration, I joined forces with Norm VanValkenburgh, a well-known land surveyor and conservation historian. By combining his perspective of Colvin's feats as Superintendent of the Adirondack Survey and my knowledge of Colvin's contributions as a gifted writer, artist, naturalist and explorer, we hoped to do him justice and make the public aware of his vision.

We formed "Friends of Verplanck Colvin" (a non-

An Extraordinary Summer

profit group) and with the donations decided on an unusual double ceremony. Two bronze plaques were cast. One was to be placed on Colvin's grave at the small town of Coeymans (south of Albany); the other at a remote site in the forest where Colvin had sur-

Bronze plaque commemorating Verplanck Colvin, "Father of the Adirondack Park," adorns a huge granite boulder at Beaver River.

veyed and left his mark. We picked Beaver River on the Stillwater Reservoir. It was an area Colvin must have liked when he was working across the Adirondacks on his long march toward the Great Corner. This crossing of several survey lines became the pivotal point for much of his enormous network. He left his initials, the date "1878," and "ADR" for Adirondack Survey on a rock at Beaver River. Our cemetery tribute took place on May 9; the Beaver River ceremony on May 16.

So who *was* Verplanck Colvin? Why did he start to dream about a big park in upstate New York? When and how? Born in Albany of a Dutch mother (the family Verplanck) and Scottish father (the family Colvin), the youngster benefited from an excellent education and his lawyer father's tutelage. He loved to roam the countryside with his childhood friend, Mills Blake, and became interested in geography and surveying. His first trip to sample the wild Adirondacks came at age 18. He was captivated. Following this, young Verplanck made three more excursions in rapid succession.

In 1868, at age 21, Colvin spoke out for the establishment of a state park and a forest preserve. He envisioned "a perpetual and refreshing summer resort for our people, and a vast natural and healthful pleasure ground for our youth...who [(will)] acquire skill and endurance..." "...at the same time, preservation of the timber and the conservation of the waters, [(will)] secure to the state vastly increased wealth, importance, and power. [(Moreover)] the continuance of the canals—the Erie, the Champlain, or the Black River—depends on the numerous rivers of the wilderness. [(Also the)] preserving from fire and destruction the vast forest which covers...5,000 square miles of northern New York."

Shortly after this speech, Colvin was elected a member of the prestigious Albany Institute. Then he was appointed to the Commission of State Parks, and later, made head of the State Land Survey, whose purpose

An Extraordinary Summer

was to survey state-owned lands in the Adirondack region. He and Mills Blake joyfully undertook this massive task in the almost 6-million-acre "howling wilderness" of upstate New York. Heading up large teams of men, with Mills as his trusted assistant, Colvin labored for 28 years (1872–1900). He produced many fine annual reports filled with surveying calculations and inventions, plus vivid prose, exquisite drawings, maps, and observations on Adirondack natural history, geology, and meteorology. Colvin probably came close to being a genius.

Surveying work took Colvin and Blake deep into the Adirondack Mountains. It showed them rare natural wonders as well as unexpected hazards. The two men thrived on the exercise, camp life, long marches, and skill in the use of rifles. They admired their fearless and independent guides and thrilled to the magnificent sunsets, rainbows, storms, and, once, the mysterious Ulloa's Rings!

Yet they endured terrible hardships as well. Hunger, winter cold, plunges through rotten ice, diarrhea, cuts and fevers, insects, heavy loads, and sore feet were commonplace ordeals. Colvin wrote in his 1886 Report: "It is safe to say, that in no other portion of [(the)] state are such...difficulties to be encountered as in the...Adirondacks."

Logistically, Colvin faced a staggering job. For one thing, he was self-taught in surveying methods. However, he did belong to many scientific and engineering organizations, including Rensselaer Polytechnic Institute (RPI), where he could discuss problems with his colleagues. Furthermore, surveying tools of that era were fairly simple and limited. Verplanck invented several instruments and techniques. Two key ones were the heliotrope and a rocket gun for sending and receiving signals to and from crews on mountain tops and along lake shores by day and night. In addition, he developed an ingenious

An Extraordinary Summer 191

method for measuring the height of mountains, and a portable canvas boat for hydrographical work.

The size of the area surveyed was also staggering. He wrote: "It is immense, this wood lot of ours. Three million acres of tangled forest in the interior occupy the centre of the district...The State of New Jersey...[(would)] fall far within the limits of...this vast northern territory. The operations of the Adirondack Survey...cover...from 3,000 to 5,000 square miles of the wilderness region....It is essentially a geodetical survey; a vast and intricate system of triangles...and thousands of miles of distances measured...for the purpose of obtaining a correct map thereof,.." Clearly this was to be his life's work.

Colvin's labor force ranged from a handful of men to almost 100, depending upon the Legislature's annual appropriation. Of necessity, Colvin hired guides (who also hunted and fished for food and made camp); packmen (each carrying 50 to 60 pounds of provisions and equipment); teamsters; boatmen and assistant surveyors. His chief assistant was Mills Blake, and his own title was superintendent of the survey.

Men were required to stay in and about camp when not working. Thirty cents a day was allotted per person for provisions (this was in 1874). Alcohol was prohibited to anyone connected with the survey. Without this strict rule, fatal accidents might have occurred, especially climbing and descending mountains.

State appropriations for the Adirondack Survey fluctuated from $1,000 in 1872 to $50,000 in 1895. Rarely did Colvin receive his salary ($5,000 a year). Many times, he had to spend personal funds to pay field expenses or publish his reports. Nevertheless, his carefully written results were published as a series of State Reports—20 in all—spanning 28 years. The

Verplanck Colvin and his trusted assistant, Mills Blake, check out a special transit outside Colvin's house in Albany.

Courtesy of: The Adirondack Museum

shortest was five pages; the longest, 617 pages. Such were the vagaries of state funding. All are collectors' items today.

Verplanck Colvin left behind a tremendous amount of accurate data. His survey lines, bench marks, corners, calculations, and maps have stood the test of time. His field notes and illustrations have earned him the reputation of an exacting, vibrant writer and artist. Most importantly, Colvin obtained a solid, factual base of true positions, distances, and ownerships so that the State could move ahead with purchases and protection of the proposed park.

Interestingly enough, researchers Dr. Steven Roecker and Dr. John Beavan, of the Rensselaer Polytechnic Institute (RPI) and Columbia University's Lamont-Doherty Earth Observatory are trying to find out whether the Adirondack Mountains are rising and expanding. Using the Global Positioning System (25 satellites and sensitive ground-based radio receivers), allows them to get incredibly accurate locations—to within 1/1000th of a meter. The scientists are measuring several peak elevations, the distances apart, and the angles between them. These data will be compared to earlier surveys, especially Colvin's work.

It's a far cry from Colvin's traditional line-of-sight surveying and his long, difficult field expeditions. Nevertheless, when his bench marks of 120-odd years ago are found and compared with today's GPS locations, Colvin's sites are amazing accurate—to within one meter!

If his bench marks have moved apart, it will mean the Adirondacks are uplifting. Some scientists predict six inches every 60 years. One practical application is determining the potential for earthquakes here.

During his 28 years of land surveys, Colvin also lobbied persistently for funding and support of his dream. He took pains to describe to the Legislature the razing of large tracts of the Adirondacks by lumbermen. This was leading to soil erosion, clogged rivers, local droughts, wild fires, and diminished water flow to the canals. In those days canals were the "thruways and northways" of New York and vital watery links to the west. Also, Colvin pointed out, certain wildlife and fishes were becoming rare or extirpated. Gradually, public and political support arose for a park.

On May 15, 1885, the Adirondack and Catskill Forest Preserves were established, followed in 1892 by the creation of the Adirondack Park (enclosed by the mythical "Blue Line", i.e. a line on a map). At the state constitutional convention of 1894, the "forever wild" clause was approved, and hence the state forest preserve and its trees were protected for all time.

Verplanck Colvin's post as Superintendent of the State Land Survey was abolished by Governor Teddy Roosevelt in 1900. The office was transferred to the U.S. Geological Survey. Two months later, Colvin's mother died. He became a bitter man. Over the next few years, he and Blake made trips to the Adirondacks to investigate a possible grand railroad line and operated some garnet mines. They did occasional surveying jobs. Colvin continued to reside in Albany. Neither man married, though Colvin confessed to once falling in love.

So what became of Colvin? And how did his park fare? In the winter of 1916–17, when he was 70 years old, Colvin slipped on the ice while running for a trolley. He hit his head and sustained a severe concussion. He became more and more incapacitated. Today it probably would have been diagnosed as a subdural hematoma with increasing pressure on the brain and could have been treated via operation. Back then there was no cure. Mills gallantly tried to nurse him at home. Eventually Colvin was declared a lunatic and committed to an asylum in Troy. There the energetic woodsman, surveyor, author, and artist weakened and wept so far from his beloved mountains. He died on May 28,

1920. This was the extraordinary end of an extraordinary New Yorker.

By the late 1960s uncontrolled land development was creeping into the Park. The Northway was being built. Large second-home complexes were starting to be constructed. In response to these changes, Governor Nelson Rockefeller named a commission to study the future of the Adirondack Park. Out of its recommendations came the creation of the Adirondack Park Agency. It released its plan for state-owned lands in 1972, and for private lands in 1973. The latter has been recognized by land-use planners as the most comprehensive regional zoning plan to regulate new development in America.

As of this writing the Park is 105 years old. There are two state-operated Visitor Interpretive Centers. The whole area plus parts of Lake Champlain have been declared a Man and Biosphere Reserve by the United Nations Environment Program as an outstanding example of temperate forest-lake-mountain environment. The largest wilderness area east of the Mississippi exists here as well. Though other state and national parks have been established over the years, the Adirondacks are still the largest park and one of the oldest, in the continental United States today.

This big, beautiful, breathtaking place is here for your pleasure and mine—free—to camp, swim, fish, canoe, ski, boat, and much more. Although the once-teeming canals are obsolete, Adirondack waters still supply millions of New Yorkers with drinking water, fishing, recreation, and tranquil scenery.

And that is why I admire this man and had planned ceremonies* for him. In the same way that John Muir is the "Father of Yosemite National Park," Verplanck

---

*Four years later, I was honored to be able to present his story to a much larger audience. The New York State Museum asked me to be a Guest Curator. I used this platform to create an exhibit, which will run to September 1998, about Colvin, titled "An Extraordinary Gift from an Extraordinary New Yorker."

An Extraordinary Summer

Colvin is the "Father of the Adirondack Park."
Thanks, Verplanck!

Afterwards, I felt quite satisfied with our centennial endeavors. I was also pleased with the sales of my new self-published book—*The Wilderness World of Anne LaBastille*—which was dedicated to the Park Centennial. The first edition was timed to come out mid-May, and it sold out rapidly.

That summer I grubbed about the farm with a light heart and spent pleasant days around my cabin. The heat continued with high humidity. When I had work to do in the barns or gardens, I waited till late in the day and on into twilight when it was cooler.

By now the barn complex was almost cleaned out. The roofs had been painted with silvery asbestos paint to reflect the sun's heat. The fine old lumber—true 2x4s, 2x8s, 2x12s, wide pine planks, tongue-and-groove paneling—was all neatly stacked in the cow barn. They don't make lumber like that anymore—cut to *exact* dimensions. I'd painted the crosspieces on the barn doors white and the big doors themselves barn red. The old tools in the workshop were sorted and a wood stove was in place. Now there was room inside to park my older truck, "Black Beauty," which I used for farm duty, and the tractor. My extra boat and trailer plus a sailboat were in the horse barn. I was proud that these once-grungy buildings finally looked presentable and were usable.

While I worked outside, I sometimes noticed strangers in pickups passing by. The drivers would stare briefly at me. With only a few houses on this road, I wondered idly where they were going. I assumed they were workmen helping with haying or repairs at my neighbors' places. I also recall late one golden evening when I stayed on hoeing in the vegetable garden and had the feeling someone or something was watching from the woods. Since the dogs didn't seem to notice anything, I put it down to those intense memories which often came to me at this hour. I picked a bunch of veggies, put it in the truck, and went inside to prepare for a trip to the cabin next dawn.

Back home it was cooler and we revived. How refreshing to swim again in the clear blue lake and to sleep in a cool green forest.

The call came at 7 A.M. next morning. It was the handyman who took care of mowing when I was away. What an odd time for him to phone, I thought.

"What's up, Jim?" I asked cheerily.

A pause.

"Somebody burned down your barns last night," he said. "Everything's gone—old truck, tractor, boats ..." his voice trailed off.

I couldn't speak.

"Hello, Anne. Anne! Are you there?"

I answered faintly. "Is the house all right? The garage?"

"Yep."

"Is the fire out?"

"Yep. Had seven fire departments here most of the night. It was a hot one. The State Police are checking it out now. You better call them."

I thanked him and hung up. Then I dialed the local station. None of the investigators were in, so I left my name and number. I sat like a stone at my desk, waiting. In a short while, a crisp older male voice called back and said, "Bureau of Criminal Investigation. Investigator Richard Sypek here. I've been checking your place and would like to ask you a few questions."

"Certainly, sir," I replied.

"Were there any old, oily rags or flammable liquids in your barns? Did they have electricity to them?"

"No, neither one. I'd almost finished cleaning and sweeping the buildings out, so there was nothing flammable like that. I was using the center part, the workshop, for storing my extra truck and riding tractor. They

An Extraordinary Summer.

had gas in them, but no cans around. No spare batteries. No hay bales in the hay loft. Really, nothing that might start a fire." Then I added, "How do you think it started?"

"Well, it began in the north barn by the inner wall and burned for some time apparently before an airliner bound for the Burlington airport saw the flaming interior. They radioed the location to the tower and then the fire departments were alerted. The men have been fighting it all night. Your farm pond is way down. Lucky it was a still night or a wind might have blown sparks across the road to your house or through the hayfields to your neighbors."

"Was anyone hurt or burned?" I asked anxiously.

"No," the investigator answered. "It would help a lot if you could come back here and talk to me."

"All right," I said feebly. "Tomorrow. What time is good for you?"

That began one of the worst nightmares of my life. There was no question in the BCI man's mind that it was arson. Based on the plane's report, he estimated the fire was started about 10:30 P.M. Yet there wasn't a scrap of evidence to link it to anyone. Arson! The hardest crime in America to prove. Ninety percent of cases go unsolved. It's a class C felony. Anyone convicted spends a long time in a big slammer.

The barn site was a scene out of Dante's inferno. Huge, blackened, hand-hewn, pegged timbers hung down dangerously from the second floor. Dozens of 12-foot-long sheets of metal roofing lay strewn about, curled and contorted from the heat like roasted claws. The milkhouse had vanished. The stacks of lumber still smoldered. "Black Beauty" was all black now and only four feet high as the tires had melted. Part of a blue down sleeping bag in back still smoked slightly. The sturdy, 18 HP, red riding tractor was a much smaller ghostly-gray vehicle.

"This place is very perilous to passersby," remarked

the investigator as we circled the ghastly remains. "You better cordon it off right away with yellow CAUTION tape and "No Trespassing" signs. If anyone gets hurt here they may sue you. You should hire a bulldozer as quickly as you can and have all the timbers and standing walls pushed together," he advised helpfully.

I stared at him amazed. "I have to do that?" my voice choked out. The enormity of the situation was just starting to penetrate my stunned brain.

Soon came the day when the remains of those two enormous, 30-foot-high, 85-year-old, Dutch gambrel-roofed buildings were pushed into one huge pyre. Then I had to strike the match that would burn them down to a low mound. The irony of that act was overpowering.

Meanwhile, curiosity seekers cruised by continually. After gawking at the arson site, they would turn around in my drive and gawk up toward the house, hoping, I suppose, to see me. Colleagues from the Adirondack Park Agency and other conservation organizations called to commiserate. (Now they were afraid). A few neighbors stopped by to cheer me up. Most of my women friends were too scared to visit. Members of the press repeatedly tried to interview me by phone and repeatedly got the story wrong. In their simplistic style of reporting news articles, it read: "An old barn in a field near Commissioner LaBastille's house burned down on the night of August 8, 1992."

This "old barn in a field" cost me tens of thousands of dollars, adding up the size and historic value of the buildings, the lumber and tools, my truck and tractor, the cleanup crews and equipment, my boats and trailer, and donations to the fire departments. Most of my fire insurance was on the house, not the barns.

I can count on one hand the true-blue friends who surfaced to help during that terrible time. They were all men. One came from near my cabin. One from Albany. Two others were my neighbor and my handyman. And the last was a total stranger who'd had his barns burned years before over a squabble and understood the turmoil I was going through.

The arson forced me to revise my definition of friendship. Level A were those acquaintances who sent out a sympathy note or called. Level B were those who actually drove by to see the disaster and console me, or sent a donation toward a reward or the cleanup. Level C were friends who physically plunged into the grimy work or psychologically helped me cope with the fear, rage, and sense of violation. C stands for Compassion! People who kept silent signified to me

My ghostly gray riding tractor sits amid charred timbers and scorched metal roofing.

they may have sided with the anti-environmental movement. They probably placed no value on natural resources, possibly failed to feel gratitude for Verplanck Colvin, and maybe could care less if this Park stays around for another 100 years. What other explanation served? How else could one explain their silence?

After I burned the barns down to ground level, a scrap metal dealer had to be hired to haul away the twisted roofing, truck, tractor, boat and trailer. But first, all the roofing—250 sheets—needed to be piled near the road. My friends and I went through plenty of new work gloves that day...little presents from me to them. Fortunately, no one got cut.

One of the hardest moments came when the scrap dealer's winch tongs descended like two huge dinosaur jaws, clamped around "Black Beauty," raised my truck, and dropped it with a resounding clatter atop the heap of steel roofing. I watched my great old Chevy, with only 110,000 miles and never an accident, disappear down the road.

Late that fall I managed to find a construction firm that could send a bulldozer to level off the debris, then cover everything over. Rains had compacted the ashes but had also softened the earth. The huge Cat got stuck, mired itself deeply, and had to be winched out. Furious with this setback, the foreman removed the Cat and left the job undone. So the eyesore lay like a black malignant patch in front of my house all winter. Off and on, snow had the grace to cover it.

A bulldozer knocks the still-standing walls and rafters into one huge pyre.

My reliable Chevy pickup ended up atop a heap of twisted metal.

In the spring, another outfit leveled the area, trucked in sand and topsoil, and seeded it with grasses. The workers did an excellent job. By autumn the only thing left to remind me of the holocaust was the square slab of concrete floor where the workshop had stood. It might make a dandy helopad someday, I thought.

Another crime took place the same night as my arson. An environmental lawyer ten miles away had his building spray-painted green—all three stories. It housed his law offices and the rental offices of the Adirondack Council, a private conservation group dedicated to the protection of the Park.

Of all the professional people in the Adirondacks,

he and I were probably the most reviled by anti-environmentalists and the most appreciated by pro-environmentalists because of our strong stances. Neither of us gave in when permit applications and legal cases threatened the Adirondacks' natural resources, or wilderness, or lake shores with over-development. After all, there was no other such park in the world. Both of us had spent eight to ten years at universities for our respective training, he in law, I in ecology. We both had advanced degrees and considerable experience. Like medical doctors we were committed to our professions and our calling to keep the environment healthy. But we paid a price.

We spent hours discussing our cases with B.C.I. Investigator Sypek and, later, Investigator Phil Arsenault. We raised $10,000 as a reward for the capture of these criminals. At Christmas time, no one claimed it. And no suspect has ever been identified.

After the fire, I avoided going to the agency for several weeks. It was a time of great fear for me. I didn't know if the same people might return to burn my house, poison my dogs, or shoot at my truck while I was traveling through the Adirondacks. Some months before, three of the APA staff had been shot at in their pickup truck while investigating a wetlands violation.

I light the fire which will burn down the remains of my two big barns to the ground.

An Extraordinary Summer

Numerous scary incidents had occurred both at APA headquarters and the Adirondack Council offices: tacks in parking lots, manure on doorsteps, intimidating phone calls, nasty signs and swastikas, and (much earlier) an attempted arson on APA's main office. It was nixed by a chance encounter between a staff member and the arsonist late at night. Those early 1990's were a time of great fear for many other environmentalists both here and across the country*.

Gradually I realized how ineffective my role would be if I stayed on at the agency. I'd be afraid to be outspoken, vote for the environment, or chair my committees. I felt like a coward to leave, for there was no other Ph.D. among the staff or the Board, and no one else trained specifically in ecology. Yet it was time to leave. It wasn't worth giving up my life. With the heaviest of hearts, after seventeen years as a commissioner appointed by the governor to do this job, I resigned. No doubt about it—this was the result the arsonists had wanted from the beginning.

That wasn't the end of my personal nightmare, however. For three and a half years, I never went out at night around the farm. I never drove anywhere or went to bed without a firearm. I never left Chekika and Xandor unattended. I never slept more than four hours a night at a stretch. I never stopped jumping at loud noises. I never stopped thinking about this assault to my professional life and the mockery it made of my environmental convictions. And I didn't write a word as a freelance writer. Until now....

On August 8, 1997, the statute of limitations will be up for both the arson of my barns and the spray-painting of the lawyer's office building. Will the perpetrators then be freed of their own fright of the past five years? What if somebody had talked?

---

*THE WAR AGAINST THE GREENS by David Helvarg, 1994, Sierra Club Books, describes many cases of harassment, violence and crimes committed against environmentalists throughout the United States.

My cabin became more of a refuge than ever. I returned there for comfort, peace, good neighbors, and safety. Thomas Merton's books were my solace. Although I still went to my farm to plant the gardens and mow the lawn in summer and spent part of each winter there, my heart was hardened to the place. I saw no more loveliness there. It had become simply a summer food supply and a winter way-station.

16

Albert

Every time I ventured into the "Bosnian bomb zone" behind my cabin, I despaired. Working alone it would take me five years, not three, to clean up from the terrible twister of July 15, 1995. Trees hit by this tornado (or microburst) leaned at every conceivable angle. Some were still standing almost straight up but had sustained structural root damage. Others leaned at a 45-degree angle, ready to drop with the next big wind. The rest lay flat like jack straws smothering the ground. It seemed that the best trees for firewood—red maple and yellow birch (hardwoods)—were pinned under balsams and spruces (softwoods) which were less efficient for heating the cabin. And it was too dangerous to try to saw them free and roll them out by myself.

In addition, great windrows of downed trees hundreds of feet long were strewn along the path of each microburst. They ran all the way back across my land to Thoreau II and beyond. Same on my neighbors' land. So far, I'd been unable to force myself through this blowdown to check my baby cabin. As many as half of all the trees in a 100,000-acre area of Adirondack forest had been toppled with their tops pointing southeast.

Worry was beginning to eat a hole in my stomach. For all I knew, Thoreau II had been flattened; or the roof ripped off; or the windows punched out by branches.

Although there was nothing of worth inside that could be ruined, the spiritual value of this quiet, small, sacred place was considerable.

But the summer was spinning by without let-up. I hadn't had any visitors who were strong enough or capable with a chain saw and axe. I would have probably pressed them into service like old-time sailors shanghaied onto her Majesty's sailing ships.

As luck would have it, I ran into my friend Albert at an Adirondack wildlife meeting. Both of us were on the board of directors, and we met every August to discuss the reintroduction and management of threatened species and to review the field research of graduate students in wildlife ecology. During lunch, I told Albert about the woeful state of affairs at West of the Wind and my fears for Thoreau II.

"I can come over to help you after Labor Day," he offered out of the blue.

I stared at him, speechless.

"I'll bring my saw and cruising axe and have that blowdown whipped into shape in no time," he said confidently.

Albert was a legend in the Adirondack Mountains. He was as powerful as a large oak. No one could match him for biological knowledge of the Park, woodslore, and his balanced view of conservation issues. Born and raised in a humble home in the woods, he had, as a youngster, fished, trapped, chopped wood, and farmed. He had also helped his guide father and post mistress mother with hundreds of tasks. His endurance grew as he walked 16 miles round trip to school. While a teenager, Albert heard about forestry as a career. He thought it would allow him to spend his life working in the woods. So he enrolled at Syracuse University's College of Forestry and Environmental Sciences. Little did he know how much more this profession would entail.

Today Albert has probably trod most major trails in the Adirondacks. He is equally at home in board rooms and at hearings where he often speaks as a key witness or expert. His work has spanned 30 years with state agencies as a forest ranger, forester, and forest preserve specialist. Albert comes as close to Colvin in his grasp of the Park as anyone I know. Now this renowned man was offering to help with my enormous woodland mess. His generosity, however, seemed too much to accept.

"No," I sighed, "I can't ask you to do that. You live too far away. It's dangerous work. You'll miss out on flying and giving your flying lessons."

"Good!" he chuckled. "I'm thinking of quitting anyway. My young students want to go flying at the strangest hours and in the craziest weather. I'm getting too old for that, but not for a little wood chopping. Besides, I've never seen your cabin."

It was true. He hadn't. "Oh, I'd love for you to visit," I replied. "Yet I don't feel right about the work, unless I can pay you for your time."

"You let me decide," he said matter-of-factly, his keen blue eyes twinkling.

So, on a warm and sunny day in mid-September, Albert showed up in the parking lot at Black Bear Lake with his neatly woven packbasket, scarred timber-cruising axe, large Stiehl chain saw, gas, oil, and a sackful of groceries and garden produce.

As I helped him into my boat, it suddenly dawned on me—Albert was another Rodney! He had the same strength, endurance, old school manners, kindness, and integrity. If Rodney had been alive, they'd be the same age—91. In fact, they'd probably be the best of friends. Just imagine if I had the *two* of them working. The blowdown would be gone in a month!

But I didn't. Rodney had cut his last tree on my land when he took down the huge dead spruce near my "companion tree." Albert and I would have to do what we could. Declining a welcoming cup of coffee, glass of water, or mid-morning snack, Albert revved up his chain saw and began to open up pathways into the tangle.

"Now we'll cut some of these balsams with their roots and dirt sticking up," he said, "then try to push or winch their bottoms back onto the ground."

One, two, three, four. Already the land looked better with those open, black pits covered over.

"See that red maple under there?" Albert pointed with a heavily gloved hand to an intertwined section of trees. "I'll free it up. You bring a peavey. We'll roll it out to block off for firewood."

Before lunch, Albert had the 18-inch-diameter maple sawed into sections. We stopped to eat, and I teased the tall woodsman about bringing a bag of groceries. "Did you think I wouldn't cook anything for you?"

He smiled and said simply, "It's how I was brought up. You keep them for my next visit. Also, I have a couple of bones for your 'wolves.'"

Shades of Rodney!

After lunch he surprised me by asking, "Would you like some of that maple split? It would dry better in halves over winter. Then you can split it with your log splitter next summer."

"Sure, if you really want to, Albert. Thanks!" I turned and headed for the cabin. "I'll bring the maul and wedge."

Albert made quick work of that, too. Legs planted firmly among the ferns, he swung the six-pound maul onto the wedge with unerring accuracy. It was all I could do to keep up with him—cutting stringers to lay on the ground, dragging the half-rounds over, and piling them up. By five o'clock we had two nice stacks covered for winter.

"Stay for supper and overnight," I invited. "It's too far to drive, and it will be dark before long."

"That's a lot of trouble for you," he said politely.

"Not at all," I replied. "I sort of planned on it. The

guest room is all set for you. Bet you're tired."

"Just a little," he admitted, as he sat down on a kitchen stool rather stiffly.

"Albert," I said, laying my head on his brawny shoulder, "You're terrific!" And I felt very safe standing next to him—safe for the first time in a long time.

We ate ravenously from a roast I'd prepared with potatoes and carrots from my farm. We soaked up the juice with a zucchini bread that Albert had baked the day before. Finally, we polished off a can of peaches in heavy syrup that he'd brought along.

"I love cold canned peaches," I remarked. "What a good meal!"

"It's the kind of supper we often had as kids growing up in the woods," he replied, "except it was venison, not beef. We raised all our own vegetables and eggs at home."

"Albert," I asked speculatively, "would you like to try to go up to my little retreat tomorrow? You should see that, too, and take a rest from sawing. But we may have to find our way through blowdown." Albert had confided that he occasionally had short spells of feeling off-balance. "We'll walk slowly and skirt around any tangles we find."

"Okay," he replied, looking pleased. "But not too early. I figure on tackling that mess here as soon as it's light."

Sure enough, at 6 A.M. I heard the swat of an axe and the thunk of a maul. Albert stood working in his heavy plaid mackinaw and size 13 leather boots, his silver hair shining in the sunrise. He didn't have so much as a pancake in his belly.

"Time for breakfast," I called.

Seated on the same kitchen stool, he unpacked and fixed his own breakfast of instant oatmeal with raisins and dried milk. "You're absolutely no trouble at all as a guest," I murmured, pouring boiling water into his bowl. He was showing me new ways to be the perfect houseguest.

"It's how I was brought up," he said in his quiet way.

"Ah," I thought to myself, "if only all American children were raised like that—and *had* to do some chores with an axe."

We started out for Thoreau II carrying two paddles and two kneeling pads to my small yellow canoe. It would take us halfway there. The land half, however, might be impassable. It took three times longer than usual to reach the tiny cabin, but neither of us fell down or banged a shin. My heart was in my throat as we covered the last 100 yards. What would we find?

To my relief the log shack was still standing. Yet a narrower escape could scarcely be imagined. When the tornado hit here, it snapped the top off of a huge dead spruce. This 25-foot-long projectile, 18 inches wide at the butt-end was flung 30 feet through the air. It zoomed over the cabin and fell on the other side, parallel to the door and totally blocking it. It had barely nicked the main roof, but its metal sheet edges and supports were smashed. I found no damage, no holes, and no structural problems with the log walls.

That spruce top was huge and branchy. I knew it would take me a couple of days to cut it up. Albert and I hadn't brought anything but his cruising axe. Instead, we looked around inside, stepped down to the lake, and made a campfire. Sitting at my outdoor log table, Albert said, "This place gives you a chance to escape the outside world and its *too many* people. You can be a real recluse here." He paused. "Good thing you had stout purlins in place. I think that's what gave the cabin strength and kept it up. I'd say Rodney did a real fine job with that roof."

In a kind of symbolic memory of my old guide friend, I'd brought hot dogs, mustard, bread, another can of peaches, and cookies—his favorite meal. Albert and I shared a Coke. He and I ate two "dogs," while Chekika and Xandor polished off the other eight. I looked up at the golden leaves and cerulean sky and felt a pleasurable glow. Albert was almost a "déjà vu" image of Rodney, except he wasn't. I was with a savvy, articulate conservationist, pilot, and colleague. I really liked that.

A few days later, I put my chain saw and food in a packbasket and struggled through the blowdowns back to Thoreau II. Most of the summer people had left Black Bear Lake and the mail boat had stopped operation many days ago. So before leaving I called Andy to say I'd be working alone up there for two days and, please, to watch for my call on return. It was prudent to let him know, since I'd be sawing, climbing atop the cabin, and hammering those roof supports. I *always* let a close friend know my whereabouts and carry a flare gun and a cell-phone for signaling.

For some reason I felt apprehensive. Would I be able to manage that huge stub alone? Fix the roof edge? Why not? I'd done plenty of repair jobs like this before. Could it be a leftover effect of the tornado? Or a loss of confidence? Or because Albert wasn't here?

Studying the stub carefully, I sawed the top off four feet down the trunk, then cut branch after branch down one side. Caution was needed because the long branches on the other side stood bent against the roof and walls. They could snap back at me or squeeze the saw blade. Every half hour or so I stopped and dragged the cut limbs into the fire ring or onto an auxiliary heap of firewood.

The job went much easier than I'd imagined. Once the branches pinned against the building were severed, the trunk fell to the ground. Then it was simply a matter of cutting up lengths of punky logs and pulling them into the woods to rot away. Amazingly, I was done by mid-afternoon.

Now that the door could be opened, I unlocked it and slipped inside. How dark and cold it felt. Then I remembered this was the first time in over a year that I'd come to work and stay overnight. Life had indeed been tumultuous lately—the arson, the tornado, and a growing issue of bigger and bigger motor boats on Black Bear Lake. I was devoting more and more time to this problem. Consequently, I'd neglected this special retreat. Yet I had built it to write, contemplate, and recharge.

I drew back the curtains, opened a window, and grabbed a broom. I swept up a squirrel-shredded kitchen towel and mouse droppings on the floor. Otherwise, the little ten-by-ten-foot place looked as inviting and peaceful as ever. Albert was right. He'd told me last week not to get so upset, jumpy, and overwhelmed by the tornado.

"Train yourself to hang on and wait," he counseled. "Time has a way of healing and life often turns right around and gets good again. You can't afford to go to pieces over one storm. *You're* the captain of the ship!"

At twilight I made a roaring fire of spruce branches and grilled steak and baked potatoes. I fed Chekika and Xandor. After dark I crawled into my sleeping bag in the loft and mused over the day. The Big Dipper made its slow circle around the North Star, and Orion edged up out of the east before dawn while I slept the sleep of hard labor well done.

Next morning I was up on the roof early, hammering new supports in place for the roof edging. I manhandled two sheets of galvanized steel up the creaky, homemade ladder and set them in place. After nailing them down and tarring over the holes, I swept fallen leaves and twigs off the entire sloping roof. As I worked, my mind mulled over the big-boats dilemma. How would it end, I wondered? Already two factions of lakeshore property owners had formed. One faction favored high-speed recreation boats for slalom and barefoot water skiing plus tandem tubing. The other group maintained that small boats and engines under

15 HP, plus self-propelled craft, were all that Black Bear Lake could handle because of its narrow width, shoals, and short length.

Eventually I stretched my achy muscles and gazed out at the lovely pond from my roof top. The jobs had been easy. The roof was ship-shape again and stronger than before. Best of all, the tiny cabin was far safer with the top of that dead spruce down and gone. A few ruddy ducks dove out on the water's lacquered blue surface. Cirrus clouds were mirrored identically—sky in pond. They promised wind and maybe rain later. The shoreline was ablaze with autumn colors interspersed with dark firs and spruces. It looked and sounded tranquil.

How lucky I was to own a sliver of shoreline on this wilderness pond in a wilderness tract where, by law, no motor boat or jet ski could ever operate, marring the smooth surface and ravishing the silence. I shrugged off these disturbing thoughts, climbed down the rickety ladder, and locked up Thoreau II. It was safe and sound and that was all that mattered.

I went back there one last time that fall strictly for "R and R"—no chain sawing, no roof sweeping—carrying my little yellow canoe up to Thoreau II. A warm spell in mid-October had the woods smelling like tangy tobacco and mushrooms from the fallen leaves. The lake had its characteristic weedy odor from the overturn, or "purge," as it is commonly called, when oxygen, water temperature, and nutrients all mix and are fairly uniform throughout the lake.

Slipping the canoe into the water, I nudged the dogs into the tippy craft and began paddling slowly along every foot of shoreline. I needed to reconnect with this lake. Chekika and Xandor fidgeted within the narrow confines until a flock of geese flew overhead, honking loudly. Then the dogs sat up and stared. In the last couple of days I'd counted 486 birds go over, mostly in flocks of 110 to 130. Perhaps a "vee" this size offered the greatest ease of flight. As always, the south-flying geese brought tears to my eyes. So many perils faced them ahead. Hunters with shotguns would be waiting in camouflaged blinds. Autumn storms, lead shot, high tension lines, and TV towers were all menacing obstacles. For every flock passing, I put my hands into a prayerful gesture and whispered skywards, "Go fast, go high, go safe. Be careful. Come back to me in the spring."

Grasses along the shore had turned tawny with frost. No signs of beavers or deer anywhere. We passed the slope with giant yellow birches where I come to get cool spring water on hot summer days. No need today. I just lowered my arm and cupped my hand to dip up cold, pungent draughts. We reached the dead tamarack skeletons standing in the water. They had died many years ago when the pond doubled its size and depth because of a new beaver dam at its outlet. Gently, I

Chekika examines a beaver lodge at wilderness pond.

paddled through the maze. The furrowed, gray textured wood had stood for over 50 years and was as tough and weatherbeaten as an old trapper's face. Impressive sculpture. What made it special today were the tiny, one-inch, two-leaved maple seedlings clinging tenaciously to clefts, stubs, crotches, *any* hint of support. They would be gaudy crimson for only two or three days. Then the leaves would drop into the water and drift away like minuscule scraps of red silk. Sink. These miniature maple torches were more spectacular than one huge flaming tree. The only eyes to admire them this autumn day in the entire Park were mine.

Later I lit a small campfire and made supper. I read at the outdoor table by one candle and waited. Absolutely no breeze. Woods as hushed as a church. Those five ruddy ducks floated and fluffed themselves soundlessly in the middle of the lake. I sensed the same equinoxial balance of mid-September now in late fall and absorbed it gratefully. Balance is something one tries to achieve over an entire lifetime. It was too dark to read anymore, so I fed the fire and waited.

At 7:30 P.M., a harvest moon appeared in the southeast. Unlike the full moons of other months—the robust orange or saffron of August, the electrical platinum of February, or the placid peach of June—this moon was dainty, diaphanous, and silvery white. It floated above the mountain top in a luminous mist. The higher it rose, the more these shimmery shawls surrounded it. Soon the ethereal orb was the size of a cloud. It drifted past the tips of sleeping spruces, trailed by shining chiffon.

The fire died down. The night chilled. I roused the dogs and we went inside Thoreau II. All night I drifted between sleepiness and wakefulness. Often I peered out to follow this elegant moon. A long time afterwards, I learned that a freak combination of ice crystals high up in the earth's atmosphere and the full moon caused this halo effect. It was a rarity. Yet for me, that night, the moon was a fairy princess. After all, hadn't those luminous veils trailed after her all night long?

Xandor lies by the campfire at Thoreau II waiting for his supper.

17

Like a Kestrel

Dawn—adazzle—conifers sparkling in the early sun with raindrop lights. Clinging to needle tips like tiny Christmas bulbs, they flash ruby, gold, chartreuse, silver, aquamarine, and emerald. The morning is fresh, clean, and fragrant. It has an innocence and timelessness that I remember from my first years here at the cabin. Years when I was innocent and timeless as well. I breathe deeply. My skin tingles in the cool August air.

Rusty blackbirds are chattering to their young in the spruce tops. They were doing the exact same thing when I was newly arrived at Black Bear Lake. Often they kept me company, flying here and there along the shoreline as I worked or read on my dock. Purple finches are warbling, too, on the balsam spires. They sound and look as winsome as ever.

One of the loons calls sweetly from out on the misty lake. Wondering where your mate is this morning? No loons lived on this lake when I moved in, and I didn't hear any for several years. Suddenly, they appeared: Nina and Verplanck. Could this still be the same pair? I think so. Loons are long-lived. They know me and my motor well, and acknowledge my presence by their trust. They approach when I call in tremolo, often fish close to my dock, and float nearby during my dawn dip. They never shriek at *my* boat when I cruise up and down the lake.

Back behind my small office two hermit thrushes are hymning, and a winter wren's song cascades out of a balsam thicket. Any day now they'll migrate. Years ago, a veery lived here. That solemn, shy songster, related to thrushes, poured out flute-like notes down the scale like a musical waterfall. Two ravens fly over, *crauk-ing* to each other. They've swooped down from the cliff near Thoreau II with their youngsters and are out on a training flight. The adults probably are the ones I've know for three decades, for ravens also live a long time. Nothing much has changed in nature, or so it seems.

Thirty years! Can it be? I moved into my cabin at Black Bear Lake on July 4, 1965 (by coincidence), just like Henry David Thoreau did at Walden Pond on July 4, 1845. Unlike Thoreau, I was afraid of many things at first. I was scared to live alone after my divorce. I was concerned because so few people came to the lake (only one older couple lived here full-time). Who could I turn to in time of trouble? Fear of assault and rape troubled my thoughts. Yet none of these worries lasted more than three weeks. They were replaced by the joy and challenge of living at the edge of wilderness. How satisfying it was to be self-reliant. I reveled in being alone and able to write or watch wildlife as long as I wished. Within the month I grew more confident that violent men would not attack me in this peaceful place, if at all. Men may question such fear, but women all over the world will recognize and relate to it.

Today? Everything's changed. I'm afraid of a whole new set of problems. I'm concerned because so many more people are coming to Black Bear Lake. Next year, summer 1997, our narrow dirt road will be paved right to the public landing and that will entice more outsiders to visit this small remote lake. Last winter the first burglary ever occurred here when two young men from outside the Park entered several vacant camps and stole guns and tools. It was rumored they did it to support a drug habit. Luckily for me, the cabins at the upper, wilder, hard-to-reach end of the lake weren't touched. What about next time?

I'm also troubled by the hostility of the big boat group. How can we convince them to act like caring members of our community and less like adolescents indulging their own whims. What if I get hit by a large powerboat or swamped by its wake while I'm in my canoe with the dogs or a guest? What if the water's dangerously cold? As the situation stands now, I fear our lake is just waiting for an accident or drowning to happen.

I worry a lot about the continued decrease in trout, frogs, deer, songbirds, and spruce trees in the Adirondacks. Big native brookies no longer rise to the lake's surface. Most have been replaced by an acid-resistant strain of hatchery-reared trout stocked every fall. Frogs, spring peepers, and salamanders at higher elevations in the Park are being wiped out by acid rain.

My dearest neighbors, who came here 40 years ago, tell me that deer often used to play and splash along the shoreline on summer evenings. I've hardly ever seen them do that, and their numbers seem low these days. Barn swallows, too, used to swoop and circle over the lake by the dozens. There are only a handful now. The tracts of large red spruce growing around our lake and other bodies of water are 30 percent to 40 percent dead. I proved this by counting them on many lakes while I researched my article for *National Geographic,* "Acid Rain—How Great A Menace?"

Not all the changes have been bad. When I started living here, very few motorboats traveled up and down the lake. Most were old clunkers that spewed a lot of gas and oil into the water. Today there are 75 runabouts with small motors and 12 large powerboats. The newer motors are more efficient and thus somewhat less polluting. However, there is still no such thing as a two-cycle marine engine with catalytic controls or devices to keep hydrocarbons from being discharged directly into the water. The U.S. Coast Guard reports 16 million motorboats and almost 1 million personal water craft are afloat in the United States today. Imagine all this pollution for pleasure!

Thirty years ago phone service, electricity, and TV didn't exist on the lake. Today they are available and most camp owners enjoy them. More affluent and professional people live here than before. There are a few new camps, and the same familiar old ones have additions, guest cottages, and sleeping shelters built to accommodate the second generation. This was bound to occur. The big change is that many owners make use of their camps from almost ice-out to almost ice-in. Formerly, folks vacationed primarily on summer weekends and during big game season. People really love this place and use it more and more. As visitor numbers and uses rise, we all need to do more to protect the environment, especially the lake, from harm. Property owners must care about clean water, healthy wildlife, silence, and ecology. *A good lake is hard to find.* It's why we're here. This should be our number one concern: keeping Black Bear unpolluted, preventing erosion and turbidity, and limiting excessive noise.

These thirty years have also brought many external changes to West of the Wind and this "ol' woodswoman." The cabin's just the same, except I added a very low basement for files and storage. The outhouse has moved 100 feet farther from the back door as I keep digging new pits. Builds character! I've also added the tiny office, a shed for my log splitter, and a new woodstove. That's about it.

Physically I'm in good shape, slim, with silvery-blond hair and plenty of energy. I notice a small loss of muscle power and an increase in achy old injuries. But these changes are compensated by knowing how to move, pace myself, and persevere. I make use of good tools and safe machinery—like a safety-feature-laden

Like a Kestrel 221

chain saw, heavy padded pants, ear muffs and helmet for sawing, a battery-operated drill, and automatic shifting and four-wheel drive in the truck. This technology has extended my ability to survive in the woods and also extended my life span, rather than being burned out like an old lumberjack at 35. It also allows me more time for watching wildlife and guiding. It lets me harness and direct my energies to write, rather than let my life force seep away on chores. Heaven knows I've wasted enough hours doing jobs the slow, hard way, and had enough accidents and pain to last this lifetime.

Now let this ol' woodswoman pound the pulpit for a few pages. Retirement, in my mind, is a fantasy for many Americans. It's not good for you. I believe that working hard your whole life, even though you may change jobs and activities often, is the way to stay fit, youthful, and tough. If you work and play outdoors as much as possible, it may help prevent cancer and heart disease. I intend to continue sawing up tornado damage, repairing buildings, stacking wood, playing with my dogs, hauling buckets of water, writing, and guiding right into my nineties—just like Albert.

There's an excitement to aging. I wouldn't go back a day. I like where I live, what I do, how I look, and what I know. The obsession with youth in our culture is sick. Over 50 and you're ready for the ash heap. Baloney! Older women should tell people forthrightly, "This is what it looks like to be 57." (Or whatever your age is.) Let your hair go grey. Remember the full moon, which I marveled at, at my baby cabin? Let your head be haloed with "silvery veils and white chiffon." It's beautiful.

Older women have the experience and maturity to offer the greatest service and skills to society of any segment of our population. They are at the peak of their promise. Look at the facts. Older women command 60 percent of the wealth in this country. They've learned much and are free to study, travel, teach, and participate in anything they wish. Child-rearing is no longer a responsibility. Women live longer. Since we're the natural care-takers in this world, I feel the greatest good that women can do is help the environmental movement. Women can save Earth's creatures and the planet.

To be effective, we must keep calm, be flexible, stay persistent in our environmental concerns. We need to feminize ecology and bring on more grass-roots activism. We should use our female powers of keen observation, extra-sensory perception, diplomacy, and persuasion.

What about men in my life? I know and work with many. I have many close male friends. Yet the few I've truly loved are gone. I'm not the only woman in this situation. I scarcely know a woman over 50 who still has a man in her life. Indeed, half of all women in America over 40 live alone. Some keep looking for the right one; others don't even want a relationship. "Life's a lot easier when you don't have to pick up after someone," a divorced friend says jokingly (except she's serious).

Women are the strong, enduring sex. As I see it, older women can't depend on older men much anymore. We can't hope that they will stay alive as long as we do, that they will always help us, be chivalrous and courteous, or even excite and pleasure us. Too much has happened. We've experienced women's liberation, equality of the sexes, harassment in the job market, loss of good manners, and much more. These phenomena have eroded relationships between women and men.

I still recall my astonishment right after the tornado when I realized that not one man had come by my camp or the camps of any other lone women at the lake to see if we were dead, alive, pinned under a tree, or needed a helping hand to clean up. Thirty years ago men would have rushed to assist women after an emergency—not just because we were women, but also because of their commitment to old, traditional, fine Adirondack values of helping out the community.

Today, some men are angry at women and their independence. How else can we explain women being battered, gang-raped, victims of sexual harassment in the armed forces, the workplace, everywhere? Some men are bullies. In their minds a woman with no man taking care of her, with only modest means, and with no power position is fair game to be bullied. My feeling is that every woman should have a position of power in her later years. She should get involved with a community activity that gives her exposure and prestige: set up a scholarship fund, get on a board of directors, help the poor and disabled, write and publish, volunteer at the library, go for a Master's degree, or guide nature walks for kids. Every woman should do something that makes her important in her eyes and her neighbors'. And if a woman spends much time alone and outdoors, I guarantee the best assets she can have today are a dog, a firearm, and an assertive attitude, posture, and walk. Be prepared. As we know, there are a few bad men out there.

Some women I know still dream about finding the "right man." Sure, he's out there. Must be at least one among the five billion people on earth. The hard part is finding him. So meanwhile we should cultivate independence and our women friends. One of the most wonderful parts of being an "ol' woodswoman" is my circle of friends—the ones who click and stick over the years. Of course it takes nurturing and patience to keep a friend. Kindness, courtesy, and correctness help and go a long way. Nothing is more comforting and enduring than friendship with a good woman.

All my friends over fifty delight me by having great things to look forward to. My oldest chum from high school just got her first dog, an elegant collie. After years in an abusive marriage, a divorce, and bouts of anxiety, now she can't wait to wake up and take her dog for a walk. Then she rushes home from work to go out with him together again. A colleague from The Explorers Club, Dr. Sylvia Earle, an oceanographer, says, "I hope to reach bottom by the year 2000." She means she plans to explore the bottom of the Pacific Ocean—in a seven-mile-deep dive. She'll be 64 and probably going deeper than any human in history. Another pal in her seventies plans three unusual trips a year, some with Elderhostel, some alone. She is a walking encyclopedia of curious geography facts. Her scrapbooks are gems of photos, maps, menus, and interesting quotes heard abroad. My colleague Dr. Eugenie Clark about whom I wrote in *Women And Wilderness,* predicts, "I plan to keep on diving and researching sharks and conserving reefs until I'm at least ninety years old." Margaret Murie, author, conservationist, and great-grandmother, who is in her nineties, is a guru to young people all over the States. She loves to help them plan careers in conservation and sort out their problems. In her late seventies she was made an honorary park ranger by the National Park Service.

Here's my last bit of advice. To anyone who dares say, "My, you're getting older," you retort, "No, I'm getting *better!*" Age? Defy it! Stay slim, strong, defiant—like a kestrel—flying into the wind.

18

Anatomy of an Eco-Catastrophe—I

The next two chapters are written for those of you all across America who are experiencing problems with larger, faster motors...be they boat engines, personal water craft, ATVs, or snowmobiles...in this rapidly changing world. Here is the case study of one small lake and its community confronted rather abruptly with big powerboats, and what we did about it. This account is intended as an academic coverage to inform and help you find ways to deal with new threats to water quality, silence, wildlife, shorelines, peace, and personal safety. Obviously there are appropriate places for large, fast motors. Just as obviously, there are places where they do not belong because of ecological and sociological constraints.

The high whine of a motorboat moved steadily up the lake. The sound bored through my log walls and closed windows. I shivered. The vibration and tone set my teeth on edge. This was no small runabout with a 10 HP engine. As it passed the cabin, I stared out and saw a large powerboat with a slalom skier cutting great swathes across the lake. It was an overcast, cool, June afternoon, and the lake was still cold, so the skier was wearing a black wet suit. As he cut each corner, an enormous "rooster tail" 12 to 15 feet high shot out to the side. Skiers only produce such spray when pulled by very large motors.

Laying aside my pad and pen, I hurried down to the

dock. As I arrived, the male loon let out a shriek of defiance. His black head and bill looked huge and his red eyes blazed with anger. He did a periscope dive, emerged like a submarine, and shrieked again. He only gave this penetrating cry when protecting his female and two newly hatched chicks. It was an uncommon sound on Black Bear Lake, where everyone loves loons. Both eggs and chicks were placed in considerable danger by such a big motorboat. The high wakes could wash eggs out of the shallow nest and into the water, or drench the chicks, causing them to chill and die. Did the male sense this as he valiantly defended his family?

The ski boat reached the upper end of the less than two-mile-long lake. How, I wondered, is it going to turn? Black Bear only averages 700 feet wide and 15 feet deep. It is crossed with shoals and clumps of big rocks, and has an island or two and many points. The boat turned and started back. The skier swung out in a wide curve. From where I stood he seemed to be dangerously close to shore. Just then the wakes from the skiboat's first pass reached my dock and set it rocking. A chair fell over. My small Alumacraft boat bucked and tugged at its painter. The outboard motor shaft bumped on the lake bottom.

Now the skier was zig-zagging back past my place. More foot-high wakes pushed onto the shore, washing as far up as the lake level during spring thaw. The waves flattened the mosses, washed out needles and duff, and ever so slightly carved into my land.

I strained to see the motor name and horsepower number of this strange new boat. To my knowledge, it had never been here before, nor had an outboard motor boat this size ever been on Black Bear Lake. But it was too far away and moving too fast for me to read name or numbers. Was it simply an outside boater who'd found the little public landing and decided to explore our lake? Or the boat of someone's guest? The one thing it could not be was a big boat belonging to a camp

Anatomy of an Eco-Catastrophe—I

owner. Our property owners' group had agreed years ago to limit horse power and ski hours.

I had no way of knowing that this single event that June afternoon in 1994 would herald the end of Black Bear Lake's peaceful summers. That it would plunge me into yet another environmental controversy. And that it would affect the well-being of our lake and community in ways no one could possibly imagine—least of all me, who had lived here close to three decades.

Next morning as I cruised down the lake to my mail box, I was puzzled to see the same big boat at a dock. I was kept too busy filling book orders that day to give it much thought. But at sunset, when I was sitting on my dock contentedly watching loons and beavers ply the placid water, the same boat purred up our lake. An entire family was aboard. It moved at five MPH close to shore with the red and green running lights glowing. An enormous American flag hung off the transom.

Slowly the truth dawned on me. This must be a camp owner's new boat. And this boat seemed to be a statement: "I am an American. I have individual rights. I'll do whatever I want on this lake."

What had gone wrong? Eight years earlier our property owners' group had voted on a voluntary Community Watercraft Resolution. Eighty-seven percent of the voters were in favor of the resolution. It read:

> *Boat motor size shall be restricted to 50 HP or less*
> *Personal water craft ("jet skis") completely banned*
> *Water ski hours 10–12 noon, 2–5 P.M.*

The group had no enforcement power whatsoever. This rule was to be obeyed based strictly on trust, respect, and neighborly good will. If someone skied on a few minutes after 5:00 P.M., a friendly gesture at a watch by a passing boater was all it took to alert the skipper. Home he or she went. If a "jet ski" happened to appear on the lake over a weekend, roaring round and round like a floating chain saw, nearby neighbors would approach the driver quietly but firmly. They'd explain that these machines were banned because Black Bear was a quiet, remote, secluded cottage lake with nesting loons.

The far-sighted individuals who had envisioned ski hours and quiet times tried to make it so that everyone could enjoy the lake. Kids could learn to ski behind 25 to 35 HP motors on small boats—that was enough power to try trick or slalom skis and even to use solo saucers and tubes. Our Watercraft Resolution also managed to give folks times to sit peacefully on their docks at sunset, or swim, canoe, sail, kayak, picnic on shore, read, sunbath, fish, loon-watch, or simply soak in the silence.

Black Bear offers unusual serenity and wildness. Few Adirondack lakes have shoreline cottages but no roads around them. Cottage owners enjoy the unique combination of no car traffic and old-fashioned Adirondack camp life. Our resolution had held big boats at bay for close to ten years. Now, apparently, the community's agreement had been defied. With that single, selfish act, all hell broke loose at Black Bear Lake.

Over the next few weeks, many neighbors discreetly and pleasantly stopped to talk to the big boat owner. They pointed out the confrontational attitude that bringing such a large motor into the boating community represented. They explained how, when the resolution took effect, the few existing boats over 50 HP had been generously "grandfathered." Yet there was an explicit understanding that when a large motor was replaced, the HP would be *down*graded to 50 HP or less. They also explained how it wouldn't be fair to those who voted for the resolution to turn around and allow this engine to remain on the lake.

Officers of the property owners' group pointed out that the New York State Navigation Law prohibits speeds of over 5 MPH within 100 feet of shore. Motor boat owners are responsible for any damages done by their boats or wakes to docks, moored craft, and property. Big boats speeding near shore could endanger

Anatomy of an Eco-Catastrophe—I

swimmers and waders, damage docks and disturb people sunning on them, and erode shorelines. The officers offered to let the association pay launch fees at a nearby marina on a much larger lake five miles away if owners would trailer their big boats over and ski there. All of these friendly, concerned lake residents were told that such a good trade-in from an old boat to this fast craft couldn't be refused for now it was possible to fast slalom and barefoot ski.

As if encouraged by the arrival of this powerboat, other big boats showed up that summer of 1994. Residents who had grandfathered big boats stepped up their use. Fast slalom skiing became a common weekend activity. Sometimes two to four boats pulling skiers and tube-riders would be on the lake at once. They all seemed to want to show off. Speeds ranged from 25 to 36 MPH. The noise intensified. The skim of hydrocarbons and greasy bubbles of motor oil detergent left behind on calm mornings seemed to stain the white buoy and plastic seagull supporting my water line darker and darker. When I took my dip at dawn, I had to scull away the thin slick of oil so it wouldn't contaminate my face and burn my eyes. Although it is true that new engines with more horsepower discharge less oil than small, old clunkers; still, the big pleasure boats on Black Bear Lake ran one to five *hours* a day; whereas the older outboards typically ran 10 to 30 *minutes*—camp to car, car to camp. Our loons screeched continually. On noisy weekend afternoons, many residents just stayed indoors or took a hike back in the woods, waiting for that blessed hour of 5 P.M. when the lake grew fairly quiet again. To their credit, the big boaters did follow the water ski hours.

In my case, it became impossible to think, create, or write. There was no stretch of tranquil hours at my writing studio on weekends, Fourth of July, Labor Day, or main vacation times. This loss of quiet time was especially irksome since I also love to waterski. For years, when Morgan and I were married and operated our hotel on that big lake, I taught the guests skiing, pulled my 180-pound husband up and down a slalom course, and perfected my own set of tricks and slalom skiing behind a 35 HP Evinrude and a small Boston whaler. Yet I'd given it up when I moved to Black Bear Lake; I thought it just too small and rocky.

Then just before Labor Day '94, two important things happened. First, out of curiosity, I volunteered to make a census of small, large, and self-propelled craft on our lake. These results surprised lots of people. I counted 75 small (12- to 14-foot) boats with 10 to 15 HP motors. They were the main transport of camp owners on our watery highway. Some camps owned two or three, and used them to haul everything imaginable. I counted 35 canoes, 15 sailboats, three kayaks, three paddle boats, and three vintage Adirondack guide boats. Clearly lake residents were into quiet, muscle-propelled water craft. As for big boats, I counted 12 to 14 with engines ranging from over 50 to 150 HP. Perhaps the biggest shock was that some horsepower numbers had been painted over or covered with stick-on numbers.

The second thing that happened was that a concerned mother with two kids and a canoe circulated a petition around the lake protesting the violation of the 1988 Watercraft Resolution. She gathered 75 signatures from lake families and their guests. The list probably represented about 70 percent of the community. She lived on the narrowest part of the lake. It measured only 400 feet wide, and big boats zoomed up and down as if they were on a race course. This woman was afraid her little tykes might get knocked over and drowned by high wakes or possibly hit by the boats if they ventured out in their paddleboat or tire tubes.

When the matter of the petition was brought up at our property owners' group on Labor Day, some people with big boats declared the signatures duplicated, fictitious, or impossible to read. They refused to acknowledge the petition. At that same meeting, I saw my first display of filibustering or stonewalling. When the officers tried to launch a serious discussion of the watercraft situation, and a solution, some people asked more and more questions. The morning wore on and folks became fidgety and hungry. Although most members had hoped that some type of plan to control big boats would be voted on, the subject was finally tabled.

The small boat users were non-plussed by such behavior. Nothing like this had ever taken place before at our simple, rustic meetings. They had been very neighborly get-togethers. The small boaters were totally unprepared, yet they quickly rallied, forming a small-boats committee, and I joined them. We now realized we needed legal help and information about what kind of ordinances or laws might protect us if the big boaters refused to remove their large boats from the lake.

The big boat advocates had also formed their own committee.

Over that winter, small boaters who had lawyer friends contacted them. The results were somewhat encouraging. They found 15 to 20 town ordinances (local laws) in New York State aimed at controlling speed and horsepower on specific lakes, ponds, or bays—for safety's sake. We also learned that any town supervisor has the authority to regulate boating and other activities to 1,500 feet from shore so as to protect the public's well-being.

On the down side, however, we discovered that New York is generally in the Dark Ages as regards state boating laws. Vermont, New Hampshire, Maine, and Maryland have much more advanced legislation. Techniques to protect lakes in these states vary from declaring them motorless or "quiet," to 5 MPH maximum speed limits, to creating very wide "No Wake" zones, to putting sensitive areas off-limits to personal water craft, by allowing car-top boats only, or regulating horsepower or speed. In New York, the only basic boating law in general that protects *lakes* is the Navigation Law specifying a 100-foot No Wake zone. The other laws protect *people* (dealing with drunken driving, registration of boats, observers in ski boats, aid in distress, and so on).

Events in the summer of 1995 startled our group. The big boats were back in force, plus a couple more. They were noisy and daring, slaloming in close to shores, docks, and swimming rafts. A 150 HP motorboat began pulling barefoot skiers at speeds of 45 to 50 MPH—the velocity necessary to support a man of 175 to 225 pounds on the surface. The boat could cover those almost-two miles of water in about one and a half minutes. It certainly made Black Bear Lake "shrink." Wakes of up to 18 inches high hit our docks and shorelines. They deepened coves and crevices already cutting into the lakeshore. The poor loons cried continually. Whenever the young loonlets were in open water, they risked being hit or driven to exhaustion—making them more vulnerable to predators such as gulls, coons and snapping turtles.

The skiing activity galvanized us into seeking out more data. Our group appointed observers around the lake to watch for water-safety violations, record the hours of heavy-duty skiing and tubing each weekend, check noise levels with a decibel meter, and take videos of big boating activity. They saw ski boats with no observers (a misdemeanor), a few near-misses as big boats swept around canoes and small boats, a swimmer almost hit by a 70 HP motorboat, and a slalom skier falling over a rock shoal.

Then a lot of bad stuff followed. Small boaters were publicly accused of having cut the underwater phone line of a big boater. One elderly neighbor chortled, "Can't you see me in wet suit, scuba tank, fins, and face mask swimming at night with clippers?" Subsequent correspondence with the repair service of the phone company revealed that the problem had been caused

Anatomy of an Eco-Catastrophe—I

when a boat prop severed the underwater cable.

I tied a white bleach bottle out to a rope and cement block in front of my dock, marking the 100-foot limit of the NYS Navigation No Wake law. It seemed necessary because an inordinate number of ski boats passed close by my land. The rope was cut free with a knife and the buoy found floating way up at the head of the lake.

At Labor Day the property owners' group assembled again for its annual meeting. Approximately 70 people—a record attendance—turned out and were seated in the parking lot beside the lake. The president was conducting business in an informal manner. As we discussed the maintenance of our community trash shed and pollution control around the lake, a large motorboat, possibly an inboard, cruised down the narrows. I turned to see who was driving. The boat made a tight curve at the lake's end and headed back. Half a minute later there was a loud thunk. Every head swiveled around. We saw a small rowboat, completely flipped over with the motor shaft sticking up in the air. The driver was bobbing in the water. Instantly half the members ran to the nearby docks to untie their boats and race to the rescue. Several ropes got tangled. My boat was the farthest over so a neighbor and I were able to shove off first and quickly arrive on the scene. The man was clinging to the wet hull and panting.

"Are you all right?" I yelled.

He nodded affirmatively as we drew up alongside. My companion grabbed the man's arms and hauled him into the boat.

"What happened?" my neighbor asked.

"I didn't take the wake right," he confessed. "Not used to maneuvering this boat since I don't get up here much. It just flipped over."

"Boy, are you lucky." I breathed out. "Supposing the boat had fallen on top of you!" Then I remembered my EMT training. "Are you sure you're not hurt? Your head wasn't hit? Anything feel broken, like ribs or arms? Is your heart acting normally?"

"Nothing feels funny," he replied after a moment. "But I do have a pacemaker."

"Oh, my God," I blurted. "It *is* waterproof, isn't it? Does it seem to be functioning?"

"Yes. I'm fine. If you'll just tow my boat to shore, I'll get it started and go home."

And that's what we did.

The meeting was a shambles after that. Some members of the big boats committee seemed reluctant to acknowledge that a big boat's wake was responsible for the accident. They wanted to strike that from the meeting's minutes. "It was his own fault for not running his boat right," was one comment.

But the truth of the matter was that, right at our meeting, we had witnessed what can happen when boats are too large and speed is imprudent on a small lake.

The community was in chaos. The issue was turning ugly. In just two years peaceful, environmentally conscious people had become polarized, hostile, and fearful. A serious undermining of the environmental protection in place had occurred. What was happening to the ground rules of democracy which is supposed to be government *of* the people, *by* the people, *for* the people, and the *greatest* good for the *greatest* number? What had become of good old-fashioned values and neighborliness? Individual freedoms can be wonderful; however, every freedom brings with it a corresponding responsibility to other individuals and to society.

19

Anatomy of an Eco-Catastrophe—II

As I stood on my dock after Labor Day, reveling in the calm, I noticed how very turbid the water appeared. In early May I could see 15 feet through the glass-clear lake. Now I couldn't see bottom at six feet. Like the people who lived on its shores, Black Bear Lake was suffering from big boats.

Studies have shown that large outboard engines (over 40 HP) can churn up water down to 15 feet, just like giant egg beaters moving up and down a lake.* In the shallows, bottom sediments are easily stirred up and resuspended into the water column. High-energy wakes washing against shorelines can add to the turbidity. Black Bear Lake averages 15 feet deep; the deepest point is only 38 feet. That meant big boat activity could account, in part, for the increase in turbidity over summer.

The potentially perilous effect of this churning became evident later that fall when I drained my cold water storage tank. As I turned it upside down for the winter, I noticed a shiny, metallic-looking, dark sludge clinging to the indentations in the 100-gallon plastic tank. I'd never seen this before.

On impulse I collected a tablespoon of sludge, put it in a small jar, and sent it to a lab for analysis. The tests showed extremely high levels of aluminum and mer-

---

*Polluting for Pleasure, by Andre Mele, 1993, W.W. Norton & Co., Inc.

cury. The mercury was twice the maximum allowed by EPA in drinking water, and the aluminum was off the charts (2,380 mg/Kg). Neither heavy metal is healthy to have in one's body. In Sweden, aluminum has been suggested as a possible cause of premature senility or possibly Alzheimer's disease. Mercury poisoning has been well documented in several countries. The lab cautioned me about drinking water from the tank or using it to make coffee or orange juice.

Where had these heavy metals come from? How did they get into my water tank?

They must have come in with the lake water. It was pumped up by a small water pump through a plastic hose suspended from a plastic buoy and seagull decoy. The intake lay half way down in ten feet of water along my shoreline. The lake water went into the water tank, and then by gravity feed to the cabin. Over summer the aluminum and mercury had obviously settled out in the tank and collected in the indentations as sludge.

That still didn't answer where the metals came from originally. From the research for my *National Geographic* article, I knew acid rain leaches many metals, nutrients, and trace elements out of soils. Mercury in Adirondack lakes is believed to be derived from mercury-bearing minerals in the soils of the lake watersheds. Aluminum can also be mobilized from soil. Those metals end up in lakes and streams, where they sift down into the bottom sediments.

Some animals in the Adirondacks have been affected by these heavy metals. Scientific studies, many by NYSDEC, show elevated concentrations of mercury in fish caught in remote lakes. The DEC advises against consumption of certain fish. But loons don't know about that. Mercury concentrations in eggs of common loons in the Adirondacks are higher than in the eggs of loons in New Hampshire and Saskatchewan. In one New York lake egg mercury levels were near those shown to cause reproductive prob-

Anatomy of an Eco-Catastrophe—II

lems in mallard ducks.

As long as a lake is relatively undisturbed, the metal-laced sediments stay on the bottom. But when motorboats pound a lake hour after hour, these sediments can be stirred up and re-enter the water column. That's how I figure the aluminum and mercury eventually reached my tank.

I know of at least eight other camp owners who drink lake water. How dangerous is it to drink such heavy metals? What are they doing to our brains and kidneys? Are we at risk?

To get more information I took samples of lake-bottom sediments the following spring, when the water was warming up but big boats hadn't begun operating. The same lab reported high levels of aluminum and mercury in the sediment—about half the amount found in the sludge concentrate. One last step was to check for heavy metals in the open lake, where the water was over 15 feet deep and the effects of the "egg beater" action would not be felt. Only a trace of both metals showed up in *that* lab analysis.

As we all know, acid rain is a major problem in parts of the Adirondacks. It will take years, or decades, to reverse the damage. The clean air laws and vehicle emission controls need to be a great deal tougher before acid rain effects on fish, trees, soils, and amphibians diminish. Can we afford to wait? The immediate solution on our lake is to curb turbidity to protect drinking water by controlling big boat speeds on this small, shallow, fragile lake.

When the big-boats committee learned of these lab results they publicly questioned whether I might have contaminated my own tank or samples of sludge.

One morning, right after Columbus Day, I started out to see my dentist. I put a few things in my boat, plus a handbag and the dogs, and cruised down to the public landing. The parking area was empty except for a large powerboat sitting on a trailer. No one in sight. I pulled my boat onto shore near the truck and let Chekika and Xandor out. They ran off to sniff, pee, and explore. This was their turf—full of rich smells of bears, coons, tires, ravens, sometimes a neat new stick to play with, and maybe another dog to meet.

I turned to pick up a box off the boat seat. Suddenly, I heard a terrible yell, "GET THOSE F―― DOGS AWAY! GET THOSE F―― DOGS AWAY!"

Where was it coming from? Who was using such profanity? I raced toward the open lot and saw a camp owner crawling out from under the trailer with a long steel wrench in his hand. Both Chekika and Xandor had discovered this stranger and were sniffing him. The man rolled onto his knees, lifted the wrench overhead, and screamed at Xandor.

The dog stood three feet away, looked at the wrench. He associated it with play time. He had never been threatened or hit. The man was going to throw a stick. But this human's body language and noises were threatening. I saw my dog hesitate, crouch down, and back up slightly. The man leaned forward. He looked ready to smash Xandor's skull.

I raced up and shouted, "Don't do it! Don't do it! He won't hurt you."

The man's face was distorted with rage, or fear, or both. I grabbed both dogs' collars and pulled them away. Chekika started barking. Xandor stood in front of me protectively. Now the man stood up, grasping the wrench in a threatening position. I spoke to him calmly, trying to reason, but words didn't register. Instead, he yelled that I was harassing him, and that I should get off the road. After a few futile attempts at pacification, I turned away. The man strode down the road, wrench still held high, and disappeared.

Weak in the knees, heart racing, I locked the dogs in the back of the truck, went back to the boat for my handbag, and then drove swiftly to town. I reported the incident to the police, but foolishly did not press

Anatomy of an Eco-Catastrophe—II

charges.

"You're sure your dogs did not bite this person?" asked the chief of police.

"Absolutely!" I answered. "They were three or four feet from the man and only trying to get his scent. Besides, my dogs are gentle, socialized, and obedience-trained. I take them everywhere—to lectures, book signings, colleges—you name it. They've never bitten anyone. I can provide written testimony from dozens of people to these facts."

"Well, there's no leash law in this township and a person is allowed to walk freely along the roads, so you didn't break any laws," the law officer concluded. "But keep a record if any more events occur."

This was the last straw in a series of unpleasant occurrences and annoyances that summer and fall. Hurriedly, I closed up my cabin that week and moved back to my farm. It was starting to look like a haven again.

Our small-boats committee was in constant communication that winter. We realized that serious ground work must be done to protect our safety, save the lake and its water quality, the loons, and community relations. We found an excellent environmental lawyer. Some people collected articles and clippings on big boat and personal water craft problems across the United States. Others delved into lake laws and analyzed the information gathered by our observers. A couple more visited environmental groups, lake associations, and biological research stations, looking for data to support our position.

Each member of our committee contributed a well-researched, reasonable article to a regional newspaper for a series entitled, "Big Boats—Small Lakes." Some were written by professional journalists and ecologists.

In March I attended a weekend workshop organized by Cornell University to teach people mediation skills and environmental conflict management. I was hoping to find a peaceful way to work with big-boat owners and salvage community spirit.

We proposed negotiation meetings between the small- and big-boat groups with paid mediators. The big boaters refused.

Finally the big-boats committee agreed to a non-mediated meeting. The small-boats proponents put forth a modest proposal. It allowed all existing big boats to stay on the lake. It called for a speed limit of 25 MPH during ski hours. Those hours would remain the same as in the past. A 15 MPH maximum speed would be required the rest of the time. The lake would have two days of "rest" each week to recover from weekend ski activities, reduce turbidity, and protect the nesting loons.

Despite six hours of discussion, no compromise was achieved. The big boaters declined the proposal.

During this winter, our group had begun to see that we were not an isolated bunch of malcontented lake residents. We were not even a single microcosm of controversy in the Adirondack Park. Big motorboats and personal water craft are a growing problem among property owners on lakes, coasts, bays, and islands all over America. People are realizing it is just as sensible to establish regulations for *powerboats* as for *automobiles*. No one questions driving a car with stop signs, red lights, speed limits, and so on. Many big boats have the same horsepower and can achieve the same speeds as cars on land, so logically they need regulations as well. So do jet skis which weigh about 400 pounds, can reach speeds of 60 MPH, make sudden turns, operate at night with lights, travel in very shallow water, and have the potential to endanger swimmers, small watercraft, waterfowl and wildlife. The Coast Guard reports that 30 percent of all pleasure boating accidents are currently caused by personal water craft.

As if to support our arguments, that summer two tragedies occurred in the Adirondacks. A woman drowned on the Fulton Chain of Lakes when she and her husband fell out of their canoe in a jumble of high wakes caused by several passing big boats. The boat drivers were never identified and probably never even realized what happened. Someone on the big-boats committee commented that it was the woman's own fault since she wore no life jacket. On Saratoga Lake, just south of the Park, where lake traffic has increased dramatically, three people were killed while operating a motorboat at high speeds (70 MPH). It impacted into some waves, flipped over, and the boat flew into pieces. Clearly, this new generation of fast powerboats needs controls.

Similar problems continued to make news. Lake Hopatcong in northern New Jersey was featured in a major article in the *New York Times,* September 5, 1995, about the conflicts between small and big boats. Fulton Chain of Lakes in the southwestern Adirondacks was forced to seek a state law and use police enforcement and patrol boat to limit speeds and decibel levels after "cigarette boats" capable of doing over 100 MPH, began operating on them. The National Park Service has banned all jet skis in Everglades and Yellowstone National Parks because these craft can frighten or kill wading birds and aquatic mammals. In the San Juan Islands of Washington State, a complete ban on personal water craft was placed by the County Commissioners. The reason? The local tourist economy of these 175 picturesque, remote islands is dependent on their artistic communities. Writers, painters, sculptors, weavers, and musicians have moved there to work because of the serene seascapes, marine life, and tranquility. That ambiance is now threatened by personal water craft darting loudly around the islands, with their drivers landing, walking on private property, then zipping away. Artists protest they cannot work and be productive with such a noisy nuisance factor.

I face the same dilemma here in the Adirondacks.

All these years at my cabin the natural beauty, healthy environment, clean water, the loons, and especially the peace, serenity, and silence have enabled me to write. My books, *National Geographic* and *Reader's Digest* pieces and other articles have brought thousands of people to the Park to experience these majestic mountains. Dozens have stayed and made it their home. My book sales help support local merchants. I've been good for the tourist economy. But now...

In the summer of 1996 the small-boats committee decided to go to a town board meeting and ask for a town ordinance. We had been stymied at every turn, though we had tried to compromise, within the lake community. Our lawyer and several property owners presented the case and requested a public hearing. They spoke for 22 minutes. A group of big boaters went on for over an hour. They announced the formation of a waterski club to educate people about how to take care of the lake and enjoy motorized water sports. No decision was reached by the board.

Meanwhile, the big boaters stated that they would not consider any law or enforcement at the lake. It was finally clear to our group that they had no intention of cooperating with the larger community, of acting in the best interest of the whole group of residents, nor of protecting the ecological health of Black Bear Lake. Every move had been a stalling action. That summer some lake residents stayed away to avoid the controversy— or from fear of retaliation. Others sadly declared that they would sell their camps.

By now our group had determined from a current taxpayer survey that 67 percent of the property owners supported a town ordinance. So we returned in October to another town board meeting, again requesting a public hearing where all the facts could be heard openly, honestly, and calmly. Nothing was decided that night either.

However, the Town wisely went ahead with its own

survey of taxpayers. It also showed that the majority of property owners want legal regulations at the lake. Our lawyer is still pressing for a public hearing in summer when the interested parties can easily attend. After that, we hope for an ordinance to bring law, order, and civility back to Black Bear Lake.

I've been embroiled in many environmental controversies, and have spent my adult life dedicated to saving wildlife, wilderness, and educating the public to appreciate nature. Among them I count the 17 years I worked at the Adirondack Park Agency reviewing permit conditions to help protect natural resources on private lands within the Park and my 24-year-campaign to save the giant grebes of Lake Atitlán, Guatemala, from extinction, which I wrote about in my book, *Mama Poc*. Later, by working with the Black Bear Lake community and local power company, I helped stop the spraying of herbicides on the right-of-way around our lake. We did not want these chemicals contaminating our springs, creeks, and lake drinking water. For the past dozen years I've volunteered and devoted part of my summertime to checking septic systems and controlling pollution around Black Bear Lake. My committee has brought a former fecal *E. coli* count of 2,400 per ml. (in a few areas) down to two bacteria per ml. Septic systems have been upgraded and our lake water became clean again.

In all these campaigns, I eventually was able to step back from the battle and see some progress, even if it was only temporary. The people I worked with on these projects were basically reasonable and interested in protecting natural resources. This big-boat problem, however, is different. It is highly volatile and highly personalized. In my case, it is disturbing my home of 30 years, making writing more difficult, destroying neighborliness, degrading drinking water, and endangering our loons. Those birds are a "species of special concern" in New York State and deserve protection.

Even more upsetting, the boat controversy has the potential to be the worst ordeal of my life. What might that be? you ask. The worst personal calamity I can envision is *if* I were forced to move away. *If* I had to say goodbye to the huge white pine, the loons, my dogs' graves, the campfire circles. . .

But this will not happen *if* people of goodwill and common sense stand firm. Not *if* human decency comes to the rescue. Not *if* democracy prevails.

20

Closing Camp

An early November day dawned mild, calm, and cloudless. Roads were dry. Temperature hovered above freezing. I leaped at the chance to drive back to Black Bear Lake and bring one last little load of belongings from my home. No matter how carefully I pack, something is always forgotten and must be retrieved. That last, fast trip is when I really "close camp."

Three hours later the dogs and I started hiking along the shoreline, not bothering to unlock the boat and wrassle the motor onto it. Five inches of soggy snow lay on the ground. A couple of miles later the dogs and I glimpsed my beloved brown cabin through the spruce trees. The place looked untouched—just as I'd left it two weeks earlier.

Slogging around a corner of the building, I sensed a change in the overcast light falling to the forest floor. I stopped, and looked up, aghast. The giant red spruce that had towered for thirty years above my cabin was gone! It lay broken in three huge sections. These sodden, smashed, grey carcasses bore no resemblance to the proud sentinel I called companion.

All thoughts of packing my forgotten items vanished as I thought back to an earlier time. Before I built my cabin, before I bought this land, before I even set foot in the Adirondacks, this tree was an eighty-foot beauty. It was one of hundreds of thousands gracing tracts of virgin woodland in this 105-year-old park. Most spruces stand straight as the masts of sailing ships. Indeed, this was a use for which many were cut in the early 1800s. This particular tree, however, had been bent while young. It had struggled to live and stand erect, slowly arched, and kept on growing.

The first time I inspected these 22 acres for sale, I noted the elegant swoop of that spruce and contemplated its commanding position on a rocky point. From here, the view flowed past huge granite rocks, over sparkling blue water, across the lake to other fir-fringed peninsulas, and eventually to low forested hills in the south. I listened to the June breeze in the tree's huge limbs. I squinted up at the glistening needles reflecting sunlight in all directions within the canopy.

How healing it would be, after my melancholy divorce, I thought, to erect a small log home next to this giant. How pleasing to extend a sun porch out to touch, perhaps encircle, that leaning trunk. How fitting to put a campfire ring and log benches near its base. And how environmentally sensitive to live without electric lines or phone cables strung through its branches. The spruce inspired these ideas. It helped me decide to purchase the property.

Moving over to where that wide base had been, I remembered how the spruce had become my carpentry assistant. I didn't wish to destroy even one square yard of the old-growth forest covering my land. As far as I could deduce, it had never been farmed, logged, pastured, burned, or built upon—it had never been anything except wild. Therefore, I ordered my cabin logs cut far away. They were trucked to the lake and dumped in the water at the lower end. Then I towed all 44 trunks over the surface with an old motorboat to my new landing. Each log was hitched by rope to the shore, like so many horses at a corral fence.

At the base of my companion tree, I fastened a king pole cut from a smaller spruce. It could pivot at the bottom on two very large screw eyes, while it swung free at its top from a rope attached to the larger spruce. Wonderingly, I kneeled down now in the snow and felt around the stump for the screw eye. It was still there.

I had added a hand winch, pulley and cable to the king pole and hung a pair of tongs on the cable's end. Then, using old-fashioned muscle power, I laboriously skidded my logs one by one from lakeshore to cabin site.

Up on the flat knoll, I had rehooked each log in the middle and raised it horizontally. A push against the kingpole, and the 16-foot, 400-pound timber would swing ponderously above the cabin base. Lowering the log, I would scrape off the bark on opposite sides and notch both ends with an axe. Finally, I rolled it on top of the lower log. Each one made another foot of cabin wall. This heavy physical toil gave me a strong sense of identity with frontier women and men—and their aching muscles.

Working this way, the tree and I had created within a month a tiny writing studio with a sleeping loft and two porches. I left the floor, roof, windows and door to professional carpenters. When completed the front porch did touch my sinewy spruce. I placed two Adirondack chairs out front and sat down to admire my companion.

Before those days I'd never taken time to study a tree and its occupants. Slowly I learned to differentiate the sound of wind soughing in the spruce tree's branches from white pines, balsam firs, and tamaracks. I stared at rain drops falling from short needles and trickling down the trunk. Over time I identified cunning brown creepers inching up the bark, rosy finches warbling in the crown, juncos, siskins, chickadees, and crossbills delicately feeding among the smaller twigs. In fall, a black-backed three-toed woodpecker rapped peremptorily on the wood. Once a martin streaked skyward up the spruce, savoring a red squirrel for supper.

Because of my growing familiarity with and affection for my companion tree, I vowed never to cut any of my big spruces or pines. I would help them grow older, encourage them to enfold me among their branches, let them accept me as part of their forest community. My big spruce taught me about faith. I stopped worrying about tall trees falling on my cabin in a wind storm and crushing me as I slept in my loft.

And that faith was tested. One winter, after I'd lived here close to 20 years, a fearsome blizzard snapped the top off my spruce about 40 feet up. That massive section sailed airily over the cabin's roof ridge, slid smoothly down the steep steel roofing, and came to rest with its pointed end on the ground. The 18-inch butt hung upon the edge of my cabin roof, causing a "dip" in the straight line of rafters and roofing. I sawed up that top, salvaging every piece for the woodstove. My spruce warmed me for several weeks.

At first, the remaining tree showed signs of life. I hoped it would send out a lateral shoot to replace its top. White pines often do and live for decades. But the injury was too great. Its life slowly faded. I began to realize how long it takes a tree to die compared to a person. Sometimes years. . .

First, a carpet of spruce needles covered the ground. Next, squirrels made off with all the cones. The outer bark slowly sloughed off. Bare branches stuck out starkly and turned silvery. Without the canopy, sparks from my campfires could shoot straight to the stars. The moon could shine down directly on the campfire benches. At last only the trunk stood in the air.

I sat down on one of those rustic benches, ripped from a log with a chain saw, and thought back to how I'd become reconciled to the skeleton of my sentinel. While it lived, I had not wanted to harm the tree. Now that it was dead, I hammered nails into the barkless

Closing Camp

sides and hung campfire grills, a barbecue fork, and a potholder on them. A rake was braced against the stump, plus long sticks for poking coals at night.

Guests still came to enjoy steak and potatoes cooked in that campfire ring. They returned home relaxed and nurtured after sitting and talking under that great snag. It never interrupted—more than I could say for some company.

Years passed. I recalled how the barren bole seemed to lean a little toward the lake; how I resisted advice from woods-wise neighbors to cut the stub down before "something happens." My rack of canoes lay nearby. The log studio was only 15 feet away. An underwater phone cable and post emerged directly in line with the leaning trunk. Still, I trusted the spruce—a lot more than some people.

By last summer, most of the bark was gone. This left dark, dry patches like leprous skin scabs. I burned scrap after scrap at night. The smooth snag no longer attracted black-backed three-toed woodpeckers. It couldn't even entice spruce bark beetles. Feeding flocks of chickadees and nuthatches stopped flitting by. That tree was down to bare bones. Yet it still stood companionably by while I strummed my guitar outdoors some evenings. While I watched tangerine sunsets reflected in mirror-still water. And while my shepherds gazed mesmerized as gentle beavers swam past.

When the tree fell, it was alone, unheard, unseen, worn out. It might even have fallen that morning, before I arrived. Never mind. Its incredible strength had defied gravity for well over a century. And, suddenly, the ramrod body had shifted 90 degrees to lie prostrate on the ground. Do trees resist this final wrenching from their roots as humans resist drifting into death?

Chilled and stiff, I got up from the bench and went back into the cold cabin to load my packbasket. I locked the door and stepped back to where the tree had stood. My spruce was gone. Yet, I thought, it can still befriend me. By its very decomposition it can teach me another lesson about life. I will purposely leave it where it fell to watch the process of gradual rot. As the spruce merges with the earth, I'll witness another phase in its energy cycle—one common to all living things.

    I, too, face old age, weakness, death, oblivion. I feel my strength has waned somewhat from when I winched stout logs up my knoll thirty years ago. As I start a fourth decade of cabin life, I would do well to reflect upon my passing. To prepare emotionally. To accept this part of the cycle with grace, wisdom, and good humor. . .even with a winsome beauty. My companion tree can teach me how.

    Instead of sawing up these sodden grey chunks of wood and heaving them into the woods, I'll wait and watch. Tiny microorganisms, saprophytes, fungi, and insects will start feeding inside those hulks. Pixie cups, mosses, mushrooms and lichens will spring from the outsides. Some spring I'll see elfin ferns and baby spruces sprouting out of this "nurse tree." They will grow greenly and energetically from the rich crumbly decaying wood. Once those layers of cambium and phloem surged with sap, water, minerals and nutrients flowing from the widely sprawling roots to the mighty branches eighty feet above the forest floor. Someday they'll support a thriving wee fairy forest.

    If I can see this botanical reincarnation take place, I can find courage. I can then truly believe that life leads to death leads to life leads to. . .I'll be buried on this much-loved wild land, not far from my companion tree and next to my shepherds. Someday I, too, will live again.

My companion tree leans toward the lake, bereft of bark and branches.
Not long after, it fell.

Epilogue

On December 29, 1996, I hiked into my cabin for that "one last load"—some photographs for this book. Despite the melancholy, foggy, rainy weather, I was happy to be going home. Stepping up to my back door, I swung the screen door open and pulled my keys out of a pocket. Reaching for the padlock, I discovered that the hasp had been forcibly pried off the door jam and it was hanging loose with the padlock. *Burglary!*

Breathless, I pushed into the kitchen and found the door to my writing studio had been similarly forced open. Close to panic, I raced outdoors to the basement door. It was ripped right off the hinges and the hasp destroyed. The door to my tool room, the door to the room housing my extensive photo collection, and the door to my basement full of writing files had also had their hasps and padlocks ripped from the jams.

The only place untouched was my woodshed.

Nothing was stolen. Nothing seemed disturbed.

Who could have committed this felony? A lost hunter seeking shelter? A thief, curiosity seeker, disgruntled reader of my books? Or...what?

And what hidden threats may still be inside? Poison, traps, a phone bug?

Or is there a "message" in this mysterious breaking and entering? Might it be a new kind of environmental intimidation? Whether it's a prankster or a predator I may never know, but surely it's the act of a coward.

As Edmund Burke (1729–1797) wrote, *"The only thing necessary for the triumph of evil is for good men to do nothing."*

Chekika and Xandor gaze at a sunset and ponder life at Black Bear Lake.